AF535101

opportunity in my community
by Winnie Christensen

Caught with My Hands Full

HAROLD SHAW PUBLISHERS WHEATON, ILLINOIS

Photo credits: Rich Ball

Library of Congress Catalog Card Number 71-133985
SBN 87788-106-5

Wheaton, Illinois 60187
Printed in United States of America

Contents

1

opportunity in my community?

"I'm not going to Bible study, Winnie," the caller on the other end of a long-distance phone declared. "I've become a militant instead!"

"A militant what?" I inquired.

"Oh, you know—I'm against the war in Vietnam, against injustice. I went to Washington to march for peace. I've decided there's a place for contemplative people like you in the world, but there are others of us who just have to *act.* In fact, that's why I'm calling now. Is there any demonstration going on in your town? If there is, I want to march in it!"

The young woman on the other end of the line had been my neighbor until a few months ago. She had come to one of our Bible-study classes regularly, and with interest. When she moved, we put her in touch with a lively Bible-study group which had recently been started in her new community.

But, as she stated on the phone, she hadn't gone to the Bible study. Now she was interested in the flare-ups of racial polarization in our town following the deaths of two black militant leaders. She would have dropped everything at home (she stopped painting the living room to phone me) to travel to our town if there had been any active protest in which she could have participated.

After talking for half an hour (it was her phone bill), she went back to painting and I returned to clearing up the lunch dishes with my back somewhat arched. I hadn't appreciated being called a "contemplative" person rather than an activist. A true accusation? *Of course not!* I thought, and I mentally shook my head with some vigor. *I acted on what I believed, didn't I?*

The inner wheels began to whirl as I thought about the problems of our immediate community. There was no doubt but that the racial rift had widened over the recent incident involving this militant group. One of the dead young men had been a local boy. Whether they agreed with him or not, the local black people could not view with indifference the death of a young man they had watched grow from childhood to an intelligent teen-ager, becoming a natural leader and an articulate spokesman for his people. His frustration with the slow progress of moderate forces had swung him into a philosophical camp which didn't apologize for its violent tactics. He came to his own violent end, still a very young man.

This is only one of the upsetting problems in our community. We also wrestle with overcrowded schools, financial crises, rising taxes, the spiraling cost of living. There are families in our town who can't put a decent meal on the table for their children. Our young men get drafted into the armed services. Sometimes they come home in coffins.

We also have our share of mental-health problems, marital breakups, lawlessness, injustice, fear. Perhaps it is the latter emotion which underrides most of the difficulties. People respond to racial issues, politics, school referendums, or any sort of change or unrest, out of the kind of fear which asks, "What will this do to me? How will it affect my children? Will they suffer for it? How will it affect my monetary investments?" *If the cost is too high, it's wrong.* Often that's the rationale of fear.

By now I was pacing the kitchen floor between table and sink, but somehow my clean-up operation was getting nowhere. Where did I fit into all of this?

I'm a suburban homemaker. I have a husband and four young children who need the presence and care of a wife and mother. I don't like war. My sons will be of draft age all too soon. I don't like injustice. I don't want my children or anyone else's children cheated out of a good education because they are a certain color, or don't speak a certain language, or live in a certain part of town. I don't like violence. I would like to send my child to school in the morning reasonably sure that he won't come home with a black eye or gash on his head, or the news that classes were terminated for the day because the sheriff's police had to move in to quell a riot. What can I, an average homemaker, *do* that is helpful and yet does not remove me from my major responsibilities at home?

The question goes even deeper than that. What is my responsibility as a *Christian* in active involvement in my community? What does Christ expect of me? Jesus Christ never expected his followers to be merely contemplative people. Their faith in him was to be lived out in meaningful action.

James said it like this:

> Be doers of the word, and not hearers only, deceiving yourselves. For if any one is a hearer of the word and not a doer, he is like a man who observes his natural face in a mirror; for he observes himself and goes away and at once forgets what he was like. But he who looks into the perfect law, the law of liberty, and perseveres, being no hearer that forgets *but a doer that acts,* he shall be blessed in his doing.[1]

King Solomon was just as succinct:

"Whatever your hand finds to do, do it with your might!"[2]

I stopped my restless pacing in the kitchen, and lifted my head in prayer: "Lord, the problems of the world are too big for me to understand, let alone cope with. I don't know where to start, even in my own community. But you do. I'm very grateful that you know exactly what's going on, and that you have everything under your control. What's more, you love and care for every single person in our town. Show me what you want me to do. I pray in your name. Amen."

2

needed: new attitudes

"*And then there was one.*" The words were flashed repeatedly on the television screen, superimposed upon a scene of happy, chaotic bedlam. The crowd flowed out of the bleachers to surround our triumphant high school basketball team—the "one" undefeated after a season's state competition. Even as the news came over radio and television, horns began to blow all over town, and carloads of teen-agers roared up and down our streets in noisy exuberance. Everyone—young and old, black and white—identified with the triumph. It was our school, our kids, our community that had reached the top. We were proud and united. It was a Good Thing.

The victory parade through town the next day spelled total enthusiasm. Drums throbbed. Bands played. Throngs of happy, cheering people spilled over the sidewalks to greet their triumphant athletes. It was a gray, overcast day, but the atmosphere was charged with excitement and warmth.

We were still charged with elation when we met with a group of Christian friends later in the day. We excitedly recounted all the events that led up to this victorious athletic achievement. The cool reaction of one of our friends to another was, "Isn't it nice that they have something to be happy about for a change, instead of complaining about riots as they usually do?"

I felt as though I had been hit hard in the pit of my stomach! These friends don't live in our community, so naturally we didn't expect them to share the same level of enthusiasm we felt; but somehow we didn't expect them to be quite so icily detached either. I guess what we had hoped for was a larger sense of community, a feeling of sharing that is wider than the boundaries of an individual town, a capacity so basic to real Christianity and yet often so markedly absent in Christians. One of the barriers we build is marked by the words, *they* and *we*. Our friends couldn't participate in our elation because we were part of that *they* group with which they wanted no identification. Yet we were all Christians. Shouldn't the feeling of *us* have come naturally?

This little incident made me stop and think and listen, especially to myself. What I say tells what I think. Even my tone of voice plainly shows my inner attitude. Jesus said,

> Out of the abundance of the heart the mouth speaks. The good man out of his good treasure brings forth good, and the evil man out of his evil treasure brings forth evil . . . on the day of judgment men will render account for every careless word they utter; for by your words you will be justified, and by your words you will be condemned.[1]

It's frightening to think that God keeps such careful records of what I say. But what has this got to do with what I *do*? Action is the subject of this book, so what difference do words make? Just this: thoughtful words as well as effective actions spring from right attitudes. If I sincerely want to be involved for Jesus Christ, I will also want whatever I say and do to stem from the right motivation and attitude.

We all need to exercise. Right? Here's this week's mental exercise: Honestly catalog everything you say for a week—and the tone of voice you use in saying it. Take note of family talk, phone conversations, group discussions. And even if you're not talking to anybody, don't register that as self-control!

In a day when bitterness, resentment, suspicion, fear and anger seem to burst from the mouths of people all around us, Christians need to be all the more careful. To "tell it like it is" is often an excuse to say just what I please without regard for the feelings or welfare of the person I'm talking to (or shouting at). In the name of protecting the purity of Christianity many Christians verbally slice each other up and down and forget that the very Christ they claim to serve was loved because of the "gracious words which proceeded out of his mouth."[2]

James goes even further and flatly states, "The anger of man does not work the righteousness of God."[3]

Are you willing to be changed? Are you willing to have your attitudes changed? This may involve having some pet security props knocked out. Human nature resists change.

A few months ago a fine young Bible teacher was conducting weekly Bible studies at our church. He had a refreshing and practical approach to the Scriptures. Discussion was lively. Enthusiasm was high. Then one Wednesday evening he showed up in class sporting a young yet healthy beard! All of a sudden people couldn't concentrate on the lesson material. All they could see was that beard, and it was disturbing.

"Hey! You forget to shave?" someone asked. Other joking, half-embarrassed comments came from members of the group, each revealing uncertainty, a loss of security. A beard just didn't fit the group pattern, and people were ill at ease not quite knowing why, or what to do about it.

Finally, the teacher, realizing the difficulty, faced it squarely. "I haven't changed, but your attitude toward me surely has. I'm the same man inside as I was a week ago. My relationship with

God is as firm and sure as it ever was. All that's different about me is that I've grown a beard. Yet, because of the slight alteration in my outward appearance, you're judging me of *changing inside*!"

Now, listen to this incident which just happened as I was writing. Today is such a gorgeous, clear, spring afternoon. You can almost see the leaves growing on the trees. The playground is filled with shouting children playing ball. Even our dog was barking exuberantly until the phone rang. The steely voice on the other end of the line threatened, "You keep that damn dog of yours quiet, or we'll burn your house down!" The receiver clicked.

I hung up the phone slowly, trying to place the voice in my mind. It had to be one of our neighbors close enough to be thoroughly bugged by our dog. That doesn't surprise me. The dog bugs me too. He just gets carried away and can't seem to quit barking. Most of the time we bring him inside so he won't bother anyone. This once I hadn't brought him in soon enough.

What troubles me is the ugliness of the threat. The caller can't separate irritation at an animal from hatred for its owner. Somehow it seems so typical of all the violent attitudes in our society. We hate people because we don't like their ideas or philosophies or clothes or manner of life. We have lost the ability to reject ideas or life-styles without rejecting the person as well.

Even though a Christian might not pick up a

gun, and his conscience might hold him back from physical violence, he'll glibly and "righteously" criticize the character and spirituality of anyone he doesn't like or understand. One evangelical minister, whose church had made a much-criticized departure from the usual pattern of operation, commented regretfully, "If you shift your methods, your theology is questioned."

The same sort of reaction is often evoked when we bring up the subject of social action. Because we have lived securely in the framework of the evangelical churches' prime responsibility to proclaim the gospel of salvation through faith in Jesus Christ, we have tended to withdraw from social involvement. When we hear in the news about poverty, we comfort ourselves with Jesus' statement of reproof "You always have the poor with you."[4] and somehow we rationalize that since this is an ever present problem in every generation, we don't need to trouble ourselves with it. We're told that two-thirds of the world is starving, but we're in no position to do much about that. Of course, we could find out about the people in our own church and community and see what their needs are, but why should we? We have to look out for ourselves. We earn our own living, mind our own business, pay our taxes. Why can't other people do the same? Why should we be responsible for their welfare?

But Jesus said, "You shall love your neighbor as yourself."[5]

James makes it even more pointed:

Dear brothers, what's the use of saying that you have faith and are Christians if you aren't proving it by helping others? Will *that* kind of faith save anyone? If you have a friend who is in need of food and clothing and you say to him, "Well, good-bye and God bless you, stay warm and eat hearty," and then don't give him clothes or food, what good does that do? So you see, it isn't enough just to have faith. You must also do good to prove that you have faith. Faith without good deeds is dead and useless.[6]

3

the church: inactive or effective?

"Personally, I feel that our church is not related to the community. We have an extensive missionary program, but we're really not doing anything in our 'immediate community.' " This honest statement came from the pastor of a local church near us. I had decided to start a search for programs of practical community help. I was looking first among local churches in the area—the logical place to begin, I thought.

The pastor went on: "In fact, I'm afraid we hide behind our big missionary budget to soothe our consciences about our lack of involvement with the people around us. Oh, we have a children's program which brings in neighborhood kids, but the emphasis is heavy on gospelizing, not socializing. I suppose one of the basic problems is that the people who attend this church don't live in this area, and so they don't feel a responsibility to the total community."

I found a similar situation echoed again and again in suburban areas. People come from outlying places to attend a particular church because they have grown up in that church, but they share little concern for the actual community in which the church is located.

An inner-city pastor, whose congregation lives in the suburbs, said, "We let church programs and meetings be a cover-up for our lack of personal involvement with people. We lack concern and compassion. We have reached the kids in our area, but not the homes. We're afraid to involve ourselves with the adults of the community, because it would disturb our pattern of life. Their ways are different. Even their vocabulary is different! Only God can break through our shells and give us new direction and a different set of values. I don't expect to see us make any inroads in this community until God changes his own people!"

As I talked to dedicated evangelical pastors I sensed a great deal of frustration at the narrow perspectives of so many of their parishioners. Many Christians feel Christ really can't work outside the rather rigidly prescribed lines they draw for him and, as a result, they spend more time building the fences of "separation" which isolate them from the world than in making meaningful contact with the people around them. Such people really don't *enjoy* Jesus Christ, nor the true liberty we have in him. As another pastor put it, "Many of the Christian parents in our church are afraid of life as it is. They are literally petrified of 'the world'! Consequently, their children aren't given the tools to meet life as it is, and an authoritarian attitude does not produce mature, thinking Christians. My primary aim as pastor here is to broaden the base and perspective of our understanding of the Word of God, to see that this is not an isolated Christianity, that we don't make our value judgments based on mere emotion but on sound biblical principles. In the framework of biblical principles we can be thoroughly involved in the needs of our community."

The concern for the church to have a more meaningful relationship in the community is shared by many pastors of both "evangelical" and "liberal" stripe, by both Catholic and Protestant. The *what* and *how* to accomplish it are the major problem. Some churches have embarked on various programs to reach the community, and I was eager to investigate them. But first I thought it might be interesting to see what an average block of homeowners in an average middle-class community thought of "the church" as a whole.

So, on a Sunday afternoon I picked a block with five homes and, armed with a fresh rose for each homeowner, plus a pad of paper, I began ringing doorbells.

In the first home lived a young couple with four preschool children and a set of grandparents, one of whom was bedridden. The house was immaculate, and the lady of the house perky and cheerful, although it was obvious she had little time to rest.

I asked her about the church they attended. She mentioned a religious affiliation, but admitted they didn't attend church much.

"Why not?" I asked.

"Churches have become too national in organization," she replied. "They're too big and too impersonal. They don't care about individuals."

"What do you mean by that?" I interjected. She thought for a moment.

"Well, for instance, my mother has been bedridden for two years. In the beginning of her illness she had to be hospitalized. Then my dad had to have a brain tumor removed and he too was hospitalized. The bills were enormous. We turned to the church for help, and there was none. We weren't quite destitute enough to qualify for their charity. Yet, all our lives we had given money to this church. We gave and gave. We were raised in church schools. This was the first time we had asked for anything in return. I guess churches are run more like a business–for profit, not for the benefit of the people. Apart from money, I asked for a minister to come and visit my mother, and in two years no one has come. They just don't seem to care."

In the next two homes the emphasis on money in the church was a major hang-up. One woman said, "We're paying on our house, educating our kids, yet we get pleas for money from a church we seldom attend to send their minister off on some trip! Yet most ministers don't even have to pay off mortgages!"

Another family echoed, "Our church doesn't know we exist until it's time for the yearly pledges to be renewed!"

Out of five families in one block, only two attended a church with any regularity. Some sent their children to Sunday school but didn't go to church themselves.

I asked, "How would you like the church workers to improve their service to you?"

In one home the quick response was, "Eliminate the money emphasis and involve themselves in my home and problems. Really care about *me*."

One mother said, "If there were only someone to talk to! I don't mean a professional psychiatrist. I just want a shoulder to cry on when the going gets rough."

Another said, "I wish the church would teach more of the Bible. Now that it's become just another social club, I get more out of Sunday morning staying at home reading my Bible for myself."

Three out of five families in one block virtually out of touch with any church. I wondered: Was this typical of all suburbia? Had communications really broken down that badly? What was missing? Why was the church so ineffective in the lives of these people?

Obviously I couldn't make any specific judgments about *their* churches. I didn't know them. But I decided to take a fresh look at the early church in the New Testament to see if I could find some answers. Who were these people in the early church? What did they do that was radically different from what is done today? Why were they so effective?

The book of Acts opens with Jesus Christ, risen from the dead, meeting with the eleven disciples. Jesus taught them tremendous things in the forty days before his ascension. His parting words were these: "You shall receive power when the Holy Spirit has come upon you; and you shall be my witnesses in Jerusalem and in all Judea and Samaria and to the end of the earth."[1] As Jesus ascended to heaven, the disciples stared into the sky until he was out of sight. Two white-robed men broke their reverie: "Men of Galilee, why are you standing here staring at the sky? Jesus has gone away to heaven, and some day, just as He went, He will return!"[2]

A new era had dawned. The disciples had work to do. They were to witness to the death and resurrection and the coming again of Jesus Christ, and they were to begin in Jerusalem.

The disciples returned to Jerusalem and held a prayer meeting in an upstairs room of the house where they were staying. Besides the disciples, there were others, including several women, Jesus' mother and his brothers. The account says, "All these *with one accord* devoted themselves to prayer."[3]

The prayer meeting lasted for several days, and the unity and harmony of the group remained intact. This was a truly remarkable achievement for such a diverse gathering of people. Mary, Jesus' mother, could so easily have pulled rank and carefully reminded the group, "I was his mother, you know." The disciples could have scolded Jesus' brothers for their disloyalty during his ministry. It was apparently not until after his resurrection that they acknowledged his deity and lordship. But the brothers were as much an accepted part of that group as were the disciples and Mary.

I doubt if we would have picked Peter as the spokesman for the group. He just didn't have "class" or tact or education. Yet he came to the foreground as the leader and spokesman, and acquired surprising eloquence.

There could have been petty rivalries, jealousies and power politics present in that upstairs room. Instead, there was perfect harmony. The one thing that united them was that each person was totally committed to Jesus Christ.

The day of Pentecost came, and they were all together in one place, "and everyone present was filled with the Holy Spirit and began speaking in languages they didn't know, for the Holy Spirit gave them this ability."[4]

The coming of the Holy Spirit had been accompanied by a roaring in the sky above the house like a great windstorm. Crowds came running to see what was happening. People from many different parts of the world were in Jerusalem at that time, and they were stunned to hear a group of Galileans speaking their native tongues so fluently.

Thus the first thing that the Holy Spirit did for the group of believers, praying in an upper room, was to give them *the ability to communicate* the message of Jesus Christ in terms which were understandable to the people around them.

I thought of the great "communications gap" which seems to separate the church from the world at large today. Is it because Christians are not filled by the Holy Spirit of God? Is the Spirit less powerful today than he was on the day of Pentecost? Then why aren't Christians communicating Jesus Christ in terms which are understandable to the people around them? Is the "generation gap" too wide for the Holy Spirit to bridge? If parents were truly filled with the Holy Spirit couldn't they communicate the living reality of Jesus Christ in recognizable terms to their children?

The old argument that only black can speak to black and white to white and rich to rich and young to young cannot be effectively supported by the example set at Pentecost. It's true that we are more likely to listen to people with whom we identify. But God is not limited by identity barriers. He can use anyone who is willing to yield to him and to be filled with the Holy Spirit, in any situation.

The message Peter preached that day to the people of all nationalities was to repent and to receive forgiveness of sins and a whole new way of life through faith in Jesus Christ. He exhorted, "Save yourselves from this crooked generation."[5]

A commitment of faith to a risen Christ (and the personal indwelling of the Holy Spirit in the life of a person who made such a commitment) was the secret for living above a society marked by corruption. Society is just as corrupt today, and the secret for rising above it is just the same. Jesus Christ lives! And his Holy Spirit has dynamic power. The problem is that *we really don't believe it.* Consequently, we don't communicate effectively. Why should we marvel when no one listens?

About three thousand responded to Peter's message that day. And this greatly enlarged group of believers in Jeus Christ "devoted themselves to the apostles' teaching and fellowship, to the breaking of bread and to prayers."[6] The fact that even greater diversity in backgrounds, nationalities and languages had been incorporated into the church didn't alter the harmony. This was a united group held together by a common faith and a common purpose, and by the Spirit himself. They worked together for a fuller understanding of the Scriptures under the teaching of the apostles. They shared responsibilities as well as privileges. This is what is implied by *fellowship.* Today we tend to limit that term to enjoying the company of people we like and get along with. But true fellowship means sharing of responsibilities as well. It doesn't allow for an attitude of "I'm sure glad that's not *my* problem." If it's the problem of a fellow Christian, then it is my problem too, because these are things we share. The early Christians had *everything* in common. They were faithful in their worship in Jesus Christ and faithful in prayer. They were aware of each other's needs and they helped each other. They were hospitable, warm, friendly. They all worked for the mutual benefit of the group. And they were perpetually thankful.

As a result of such living, dynamic faith, miracles began to happen. People started to take notice. This kind of living was not the norm in that society. Many more people believed in Jesus Christ. And the church grew.

What a different story the church seems to tell today. We're struggling to unite. We're sophisticated, organized structures—and dead. But there's hope for a resurgence of life if each person makes a fresh commitment of his life to the risen Christ and allows the Holy Spirit to fill him. This may produce some drastic changes, but won't it be worth it?

This is how the apostle Paul, described the whole framework for the life and function of the church in the world today:

> Now is the time to cast off and throw away all these rotten garments of anger, hatred, cursing, and dirty language. Don't tell lies to

each other; it was your old life with all its wickedness that did that sort of thing; now it is dead and gone. You are living a brand new kind of life that is continually learning more and more of what is right, and trying constantly to be more and more like Christ who created this new life within you.

In this new life one's nationality or race or education or social position is unimportant; such things mean nothing. Whether a person has Christ is what matters, and He is equally available to all.

Since you have been chosen by God who has given you this new kind of life, and because of His deep love and concern for you, you should practice tenderhearted mercy and kindness to others. Don't worry about making a good impression on them but be ready to suffer quietly and patiently.

Be gentle and ready to forgive; never hold grudges. Remember, the Lord forgave you, so you must forgive others.

Most of all, let love guide your life for then the whole church will stay together in perfect harmony.

Let the peace of heart which comes from Christ be always present in your hearts and lives, for this is your responsibility and privilege as members of His body. And always be thankful.

Remember what Christ taught and let His

> words enrich your lives and make you wise; teach them to each other and sing them out in psalms and hymns and spiritual songs, singing to the Lord with thankful hearts.
>
> And whatever you do or say, let it be as a representative of the Lord Jesus, and come with Him into the presence of God the Father to give Him your thanks.[7]

"You can't imagine what a nice feeling it is to go to church any night of the week and find the place swarming with people," said a young lawyer as he described the open-door policy of his church. "Our church is operated as an open institution," he went on. "It's always unlocked. All kinds of people use the church for a meeting place, from political organizations to Alcoholics Anonymous. These aren't church-sponsored groups, but they need a place to meet, so we share our facilities."

I questioned a number of pastors as well as laymen in both the inner city and the suburbs to see what specific programs each church offered for meeting the basic social needs of the people in their communities. In what practical ways other than church services were the churches trying to relate to the people around them?

Many churches become polling places during election time. Others with good educational facilities invite the presence of special classes for the handicapped or Head Start programs for preschoolers. One suburban pastor I talked to is anxious to get a day-care center started for mothers who have to work but can't afford the cost of regular nursery schools for their children. The local director of the office of economic opportunity in our community said, "We could use the facilities of local churches to feed breakfast to the deprived children of the community."

Some churches with recreational facilities operate programs for the youth of the community whether they attend the church or not. Another church is opening one of its wings to establish a job-training center for the community where typing, shorthand, sewing, key-punch operating, and other job skills will be taught.

Imagine entertaining fifty teen-agers in your home every week! A godly woman in our church did that. The high school group met in her beautifully furnished living room. She admitted that she often viewed with dismay the beating her furniture was taking from this enthusiastic and active group of young people. Then one day she read the verse in her Bible, "And [you] took joyfully the spoiling of your goods."[8]

After that, she didn't worry about the furniture and the rugs wearing out with so much traffic. She accepted it joyfully. And her generous attitude has paid off well. To this day men and women, sometimes from great distances, write to her. Many of them were introduced to Jesus Christ in her living room.

A Christian home or a church building should never be used just for the comfort and benefit of the owners. All that we have is a trust from God to be shared with others. The apostle Paul states it quite simply: "Practice hospitality."[9] And Peter adds that we should do it "ungrudgingly."[10] In spite of these injunctions, there are lovely homes where no one but close friends and family is welcome, and many churches with splendid, modern, educational facilities that are actually used only three or four hours of the week, and then only for members of the congregation.

"Whatever we have, we share with our community," said Miss Marjorie Branch, whose full-time employment is with the Chicago Board of Education and who volunteers her time as director of education at an inner-city church.

My fourteen-year-old son and I visited the church on a Sunday afternoon to see the weekly tutoring program they sponsor. We parked in a dead-end street behind the church. Attached to its back wall was a battered basketball hoop. The street was bordered by an alley piled high with garbage and broken bottles, and filled with potholes. Whenever a car needed to turn around, it was necessary to drive into the alley and back up through the "basketball court" before driving out. When we did so, the basketball players had to flatten themselves against the church wall to avoid being hit. My son, whose first love is basketball (when it's in season) was stunned by the limited facilities which these boys had. The tutoring program is held in the church basement. There are the usual round posts and poor lighting, familiar in an old building. But colorful posters on the walls relate to themes of "peace" and "love" and "joy." Miss Branch greets tutors and students alike with warm and shining enthusiasm. The atmosphere clearly says, "Learning is fun, not a drag." Each child is given the same tutor each week. The teaching materials used are designed to supplement rather than duplicate what the children might get in school. "However, there is a real dearth here of materials related to our urban youth," Miss Branch commented.

The tutors, all white and mostly from widely scattered suburban communities, are asked to attend services at this inner-city church to develop a measure of identification with the community.

"The tutoring program began," said one of the staff members, "when we realized that the children in our Sunday school couldn't read. You can't get far in teaching the Bible when the children can't read it. So we began the remedial reading program for the benefit of our own Sunday school children. Now it includes anyone in the neighborhood who wants to come. It has been advertised in the public schools in the area. There are 11,000 children in the church vicinity. I would estimate that 10,500 of them need remedial reading."

The tutoring effort of this one church hardly scratches the surface of the overall need. The program is only one hour a week and affects perhaps forty or fifty students. Not much. But it's better than nothing. The results have been rewarding. Parents appreciate the concern and time taken with their children. It has given the church acceptance in the community. More than that, children have learned to read.

Lack of reading skills is not necessarily limited to the inner city. Suburban communities have similar difficulties. In one suburb the tutors pick up their students from their homes and take them to their own homes for dinner as well as a lesson. The teaching is a team effort between parents, schoolteachers, and tutors. Cultural and spiritual, as well as educational, barriers are bridged.

As we drove home, my son remarked, "It's hard to realize so many kids live like that."

Yes, it is. It's even harder to realize that in a country where technology has sent man to the moon, so many children can't read the simplest primers. I wondered about the children in our community. What was their reading level? I honestly didn't know.

I had never taken the time to find out.

How about your community? We send missionaries to tribes who have no written language. *But we have a written language.* The written Word of God is basic to Christianity. The Christian church is responsible not only to convey the gospel message orally but also to share the basic tools by which each person can discover these truths for himself.

4

the crippled city

Have you ever thought what it would be like to be a cripple?

A familiar sight at our local shopping center in the warmer months of the year is a man who sits on the ground outside a busy store with his short, useless, deformed legs stretched out in front of him. In his hand is a container for pennies, dimes, quarters. I have often wondered what goes through people's minds as they pass this helpless figure.

Some are pitiers. This is probably the largest group—those who have a sincere sense of pity for someone so unfortunate. Pitying people pull out coins and drop them into the container and are momentarily grateful that they have healthy legs. Such a pity. Poor thing. And on they rush. As soon as the cripple is out of sight he isn't given another thought.

Then there are the indifferent—those too busy or preoccupied to notice. They may be hardened pitiers—people who have passed the man so many times, dropped coins, and feel no more sense of obligation. They have done their share.

Then there are the escapists—those who don't want to see anything ugly or abnormal. They are repulsed by it or find it too disturbing. They look away deliberately, refusing to see the man and his plight. They can almost convince themselves he doesn't exist at all. "If I don't see him, he's not really there." This kind of reasoning may sound ridiculous when it's spelled out, but it is all too real in our actions and rationalizations. In so many areas of life we run from problems rather than face them. If a marriage gets rocky: divorce. If a job isn't to my liking: quit. If my community develops problems: move. If I have problems within myself: take refuge in depression, drugs, alcohol, or blame it on circumstances or someone else—anything but face myself and my problems.

Others are skeptics. They say, "There are all kinds of jobs for handicapped people. No one needs to beg. Why doesn't he go find a job?" Such people never take the time to find out the particulars. Perhaps the man has tried, but has no transportation. Maybe he doesn't have the necessary skills. Maybe there are no jobs available. The skeptic scorns but doesn't investigate.

But some really care. There may be only one, who knows that man well enough to bring him to this spot each day, and to take him home again at night. Hopefully, that person cares enough to know the man's real problems and needs, what he thinks, how he feels.

But what about the cripple's own reaction to his lot in life? Does he envy the hundreds of healthy legs moving past him? Does he resent the fact that most people take their strong legs for granted? He sits helplessly even in the wind and rain till someone moves him. Does he resent being so totally dependent on others? Is he grateful for the contributions, or does he feel society owes him this because life cheated him so badly?

All these thoughts came tumbling through my mind one afternoon when I was in the plaza shopping with my eleven-year-old daughter. As usual, I was in a rush. We needed shoes, and were having difficulty finding the right size. Going from one store to another, we passed the cripple, seated as usual on the sidewalk. I felt quickly in my purse for change and couldn't find any, only a checkbook and charge cards. But as we walked by I gave the man as warm a smile as I could muster. His immediate response to my friendly glance was to lift his cup and rattle it at me. He wanted more than a smile. In my discomfort I looked away and hurried by. I didn't know how to cope with the situation, so it was easier to leave as quickly as possible!

There isn't a person alive, handicapped or normal, who wants to be forgotten or ignored. But the more people there are, the more impersonal society becomes. From birth to death, people are recorded as little square holes on somebody's computer card. They are no longer personalities but numbers punched out on a card. The original student unrest at Berkeley University was a revolt against the impersonal machinery which bound the student population. Many classes were conducted by closed-circuit TV. The students never saw their professors in person. They didn't appreciate being numbers. They wanted to be heard and treated as people. Cups began to rattle. Voices. Marches. Sit-ins. Rhetoric. The issues became more pressing. The cups got larger. The rattle louder. Rocks. Obscenities. Fire. Shots. Bombs. Strikes. Anything to shake a complacent, indifferent, materialistic society into awareness and action, or reaction.

Among the major "cripples" calling for attention today are our nation's cities. Our family moved out of the city when we bought our first home. Although my husband works in the city, we have felt little attachment or responsibility toward it. Frequently, in driving into town, the comment from some member of the family has been, "Boy, am I glad we don't live here!" We felt little identification with this huge, sprawling, dirty metropolis and were relieved not to be part of it. Then cups began rattling, and suburbanites began to awaken to the fact that urban problems were not so far removed as they thought they were.

Our nation's former Vice-President, Hubert

Humphrey, in a speech to the Congress of the Cities in Boston on August 7, 1967, defined the national problem in this way:

> We are an urban nation. Seventy percent of our people now live in cities, and the figures indicate that by the year 1977, eighty percent of our people will be living in cities. What happens in our cities happens to America. It is by the quality of life in our cities that the character of our civilization will be judged. It is in our cities that American democracy will either succeed or fail, survive or perish.[1]

He went on to say,

> This is a time in our history when we must squarely face up to the responsibilities of American citizenship. We all jealously guard our rights as Americans. We point with great pride to the abundance of our national economy. But every right carries with it a commensurate responsibility. There is no freedom without duty. There is no role of leadership without responsibility. As our rights expand, our material wealth increases, so also do the responsibilities, and the duties, not just of governmental officials, but of *every* American.[2]

The day has long passed when the suburbanite could comfortably ride out of the city on the commuter train and ignore the helplessness, decay and heartache whizzing by his window. Someone has said that the day of the megalopolis is not far away. Cities, suburbs, towns, villages will then be merged into one giant complex. How far out can a person run to avoid involvement with the problems of the inner city?

If all citizens should be concerned, Christians should be particularly concerned.

I heard the sardonic comment, "I think we should bring home all the missionaries we have sent 'to the ends of the earth,' because we're doing such a rotten job in 'Jerusalem.' "

A brilliant young lawyer who lives and works in Chicago, and who donates a great deal of his time and legal services to representing deprived and exploited people, said, "Chicago is a very small town when you get involved. You keep meeting the same small group of concerned people all over the city. They seem to be the only ones who care."

What can the evangelical Christian do about the problems of the inner city? Dr. Howard Hageman, pastor of the North Reformed Church in Newark, New Jersey, who has worked for twenty-four years in that city, said,

> First of all, if we are going to be effective witnesses in the inner city, we had best get over the . . . hang-up we have about working in the ghetto. I have no sympathy whatever with those who claim that hunger, poverty, bad education and bad housing are simply social questions with which the church should not be concerned. . . .[Second,] I

> cannot possibly hope to speak meaningfully about Christ to the people in the inner city if I have not been with them in their struggles for decency, dignity, and human welfare. If after the battle is all over, I walk in and say I want to speak about Jesus Christ, they simply will not listen! "Where were you and your Christ when we needed you?" will be their inevitable response. And to me at least that is almost an unanswerable question. The Christ in whom I believe is concerned about human wholeness, the needs of the body.[3]

A Christian lawyer who lives in the inner city is often called on to represent gang members when they get in trouble. Because he is willing to get involved in this way with the needs of people, they are more responsive to what he has to say about Christ, as he has opportunity.

A pastor and his wife and young children decided to move back into the city from their comfortable home in the suburbs. They got an apartment in a typically old building. There had been riots in that very area just before they moved. The wife admitted that at first she was so frightened that she lost fifteen pounds. But as they got settled in she felt more at home and rapidly regained the lost weight! This young minister walks the streets, talking to the people in the ghettos, frequenting hippie hangouts, and talking to kids who have "dropped out" or run away from home.

Dick and Audrey, another couple I talked to, chose to remain in the city rather than move out. They have five children. Audrey, a nurse, is often called on by her neighbors for emergencies or even to read a thermometer for an illiterate mother. She talked of the advantages of city life. "For one thing, it is cheaper. Taxes are lower. My husband doesn't have to hold two jobs to 'keep up.' This gives us more time with our children. Another thing–our well-functioning, loving family life makes an impression in the community where family living is not the rule. Other families don't work together. Also, I don't feel our children are being cheated educationally. It takes more of our time as parents to supplement their education, but it's well worth it. We're happy in the city because God put us here."

A Christian teacher who teaches in the city but lives in the suburbs admitted that he came to the sickening realization one day that in nine years of teaching he did not really know one local resident or businessman in the vicinity of the school. He decided to remedy this deficiency and is now participating in a local ministry to alienated youth in a "dirty little yellow 'haunted' house."

Mrs. Jones is also a teacher. She was a former missionary in a foreign country. She decided to make a ghetto school her mission field. The first few days she came home from classes covered with bruises from books and other things which the students had thrown at her. Her arms were black and blue. Then one morning she brought a Bible to the classroom. She raised it high for all to see, and asked, "How many of you know what this book is?" Only one child in the room could identify it.

"Well, I'm going to read to you from it every day," she said. And she did. As a result of daily Bible reading, the discipline problem gradually subsided and she had a more orderly classroom.

Another Christian teacher in the ghetto visits the homes of her pupils after hours. She collects clothes for her students who have little to wear. Under school auspices, she also takes children camping to teach them the wonders of nature, an aspect of life largely absent in the concrete and filth of the inner city.

Another group of Christians is working with the city on low-income housing. They are taking advantage of both state and federal funds to sponsor an apartment building for low-income elderly people. They are also planning family units.

The American Bible Society recently conducted an experiment in Chicago. They chose a five-block area in the district with the highest crime rate in Chicago, and flooded the area with 7,000 gospels of John, enclosing an invitation for anyone who wanted more reading material to send for a free copy of Luke or, for twenty-five cents, the whole New Testament in modern English. They received two-hundred requests for New Testaments in response to the mailing. More significant to them was the fact that the police captain in the district reported that the crime rate had dropped drastically in one month's time. The same experiment was conducted in another area with a high crime rate, with a similar result. If just mailing the Scriptures can have such a dramatic effect, think of what could be accomplished with a person-to-person contact with the people who were interested enough to ask for more. If Christians lived in the area, there would be prospects for at least twenty Bible-study groups!

The apostles Peter and John met a cripple one day on their way to church. As Peter and John were going into the building, the cripple asked for a contribution. Perhaps he rattled his cup at them. They stopped and looked at the helpless man. Then Peter said, "We don't have any money for you! But I'll give you something else! I command you in the name of Jesus Christ of Nazareth, *walk*!" What a dramatic moment! Peter was offering to this man, in the name of Christ, something no amount of money could have purchased —two healthy legs. It's often a good thing *not* to have money to give. It's often too easy to write a check or make a donation and feel we have done our bit for humanity. It's good to give money, but it should never stop there.

Peter did not turn, then, and go into the temple. If he had, the man might never have stood up. Instead, Peter "*took him by the right hand and raised him up*; and immediately his feet and ankles were made strong." This man, who had never taken a step in his life, went leaping and walking into the temple, praising God! Peter didn't just say "Christ is your answer" or put a tract in his hand and walk away. He stayed and became personally involved in helping that man get to his feet. And it was in the process of pulling him up that the strength came to his ankles. Who had released him from the bondage of a lifetime? Jesus Christ. Christ was his answer. But he would never have found this answer if one of Christ's messengers hadn't stopped and become personally involved.

"How lonely sits the city. . . . All her people groan as they search for bread. . . . Is it nothing to you, all you who pass by?"[6]

5

". . . in prison,
and
you came."

The county jail is an old building. Apart from necessity or mission, it is not a pleasant place to visit. I was there with the Protestant chaplain's wife and another lady to see the rehabilitation building which had recently been built in one of the small open areas between wings of the jail.

We walked through the lobby in which people (and most of them seemed young) were waiting to visit inmates, then up a flight of stairs to a locked door. Satisfied as to our identity, the guard unlocked the door, let us in, and immediately locked the door again behind us. The first thing that struck me were the bars. There were so many of them. The record-keeping department was all behind bars. So were the jail staff and their desks and file cabinets. Down the hall we could see the cell-blocks behind several series of bars. There were visitors' cubicles, and areas in which the inmates could consult their lawyers. These too had separating bars. As we stood in the corridor, the only place freely open to access was the superintendent's office.

When the chaplain was free to take us on the tour of the buildings, Phyllis, the third member of our party, turned to me and asked,

"Have you been here before?"

"Yes," I replied, "but it was a long time ago. Our high school class had a field trip here. All I remember from that visit was the electric chair!"

"Well, that's gone," Phyllis said. "But my first trip down here a few months ago was probably the biggest cultural shock of my life."

I could understand her feeling. It wasn't that the jail was filthy. It wasn't. Nor were the guards loud and cruel; at the least, not in our presence. It was just the sense of dehumanization in looking through the bars and seeing groups of grown men in their 40's and 50's just sitting and staring into space or wandering aimlessly around the dayroom. They sat by the hour. The younger men were in a different cellblock, but their limit of activity was the same.

Cook County Jail handles an average of 24,000 persons a year. Inmates are there for sentences of no more than one year, so the traffic in and out is heavy. The building is overcrowded; the facilities for recreation or rehabilitation are limited. Consequently, the inmate has plenty of idle time on his hands and this time is "most likely to be used negatively in harboring grievances, building grudges, planning for revenge, and learning 'tricks of the trade' from those already seasoned in the criminal subculture," according to Chaplain John Erwin.

It was not only the idle time which was of concern to Chaplain Erwin, but also the fact that "most of the prisoners come from the inner city and have had little or no success at the normal pursuits of life." Many of them are unskilled in any kind of occupation. Seventy-seven percent of the inmates were not working at the time of their arrest. Educationally, more than 50 percent have less than ten years of formal education and 16.7 percent have completed only eight years of school. One of every four inmates is a functional illiterate. Illiteracy, lack of vocational ability, and emotional immaturity are all contributing factors to the 75 percent return rate of convicts to prison after their release.

Chaplain Erwin emerged from the superintendent's office to show us the rehabilitation facilities that were the product of his dreams and hard work.

"It's not enough to get a man saved," he said as we walked to the elevator, "if he doesn't know how to read or have some kind of trade when he leaves here. We have men who would like to work but can't read well enough even to fill out a job-application form."

This adult illiteracy moved Chaplain Erwin to start an experimental educational program for jail inmates which is now known as PACE Institute (Programmed Activities for Correctional Education). To interested inmates PACE offers opportunities to learn to read, or to fill out the missing areas of their education from the point at which they dropped out of school.

The building housing PACE Institute is the newest section of Cook County Jail. It isn't elaborate, but it's new, brightly painted, and even the bars on the windows are decorative! When we walked in, a group of about forty inmates was listening closely to a representative of a local junior college telling of the special program their school offers to former inmates. Of special interest to the men was the cost (they could apply for certain government grants) and the fact that special provisions were made for those who lacked high school diplomas.

Beside basic education, inmates are also offered vocational training in keeping with their interests and abilities. A large room housing an automobile engine, power tools, worktables, drawing boards, and other equipment, is the place used for developing manual skills. Four young men (they all looked under twenty years of age) turned as we came in. One was sitting at a drawing board. In a few minutes of conversation it was quite apparent that their enthusiasm ran high for this program. One young man was setting out to become a carpenter, another was interested in the tool-and-die industry, another in mechanics. "Actually, we probably learn more here than kids in high school," commented one inmate, "because every fellow in this program *wants* to learn. No one is forcing him."

It is important for a man to change his attitude toward society and toward himself. He has to have a feeling of self-worth. "Only Christ can change a man within," admits Chaplain Erwin, "but Christ was interested in the whole person. And what we try to do is minister to the whole man. We could use Christian men here, who would be willing to share their skills and trades. But, even more than that, we need those who would care enough just to make friends with these men on a one-to-one basis, and then continue the personal contacts after they get out."

Ruth and Bob were two such people who gave of themselves. They were not educators nor professionals. They were typical suburbanites with four young children. They started going to jail to paint.

"I hate to paint!" Ruth laughed as she recounted their experience, "but we heard that Chaplain Erwin needed help, so Bob and I came to help. We painted, laid tile, put in ceilings, and loved every minute of it."

Ruth's husband, Bob, is an executive in a large department store, but he changed into old clothes and went to the jail after office hours night after night to work.

Inmates also volunteered to help. One of them was Tony. He had a prison record spanning back eighteen years. A drug addict, he usually landed in jail for stealing to support his habit. Over the months he developed a great respect for the Christian character and integrity of the chaplain, John Erwin.

When Tony showed up on the work detail the chaplain said, "Oh, no not him!" Tony had quite a reputation as a "con artist." But Tony it was, and Tony worked hard, side by side with Ruth and Bob. He talked to them by the hour as they hammered, painted and laid tile. He had never met people like these. Imagine, an executive, on his hands and knees doing menial work! Why, even the chaplain was there in work clothes working until midnight.

Tony had met Christians before who had tried to beat him over the head with the Bible. They would preach and talk and hand out tracts and leave, but these people showed they really *cared* about men like him. Tony asked Ruth and Bob a lot of questions while they worked. They talked about Christ and the Bible, but it was different with a paint brush in their hands. This was *living* Christianity.

After many conversations, Ruth asked Tony, "Have you ever thought about accepting Christ?"

"Yes," replied Tony, "but I don't know how." Ruth sent him a New Testament and told him to read John, chapter 3. Tony did. But he didn't accept Christ until the day he was released from prison. "I purposely held off," he said, "to show that I really meant business. I didn't want anyone to think I believed just to get special favors while still in prison."

Tony made a profession of faith in Christ because people who *lived* their Christianity had communicated Christ to him.

The apostle Paul said, "The kingdom of God is not just talking: it is living by God's power."[1] Now, the real test comes for Tony as he establishes life again on the "outside." Ruth and Bob will keep in touch with him, but this is a critical transition period. And Chaplain Erwin wishes there were a good halfway house to which people like Tony could be referred. Many communities have established halfway houses to help rehabilitate prison inmates after their release. In these homes there is still a measure of regimentation, helpful guidance in finding work, establishing responsibility. When such houses are staffed by Christians, spiritual undergirding can be added. We all like "instant success" stories. There can be success, but it usually takes time, involvement, patience, and lots of faith.

I thought of the apostle Paul's own experience in jail. People forgot him. They were ashamed of his chains. He longed for his friends. "Luke alone is with me," he wrote to Timothy.[2] And he reminded Timothy that he was "a whole person" when he asked for his coat and his books. His body and mind needed care just as did his spirit. If Paul, a spiritual giant, longed for the personal attention and presence and care of his friends, how much more does the person who has never met Jesus Christ.

Jesus said, "I was in prison and you came to me. . . . As you did it to one of the least of these my brethren, you did it to me."[3]

One of Paul's friends, Onesiphorus, had a hard time finding him in Rome. But he kept up the search until he did, and his visit revived Paul "like a breath of fresh air."[4]

being black

"Read, Baby, Read" was the caption cross the top of the printed sheet handed to each person who entered the arena for the crusade. We were attending an integrated evangelistic crusade conducted by the black evangelist, Tom Skinner. The printed sheet we received, along with other program materials, was actually a reprint of an article by Lois M. Ottaway in *Christianity Today,* suggesting that a first step in attempting to understand the racial crisis is to read books which would enlighten the white person on the black man—his history, his way of life, his needs, his problems.

"One cannot begin to understand others until he begins to feel with them, to gain insight into their lives, and to respect them," says Miss Ottaway. To the concerned white American who asks, "What can I do?" she replies, "Try to learn what it is like to be a black in white America . . . read!" I glanced through the list of suggested books and noted with some satisfaction that I had read a good number of them. It hadn't been a pleasant experience, but it had been enlightening.

Reading can provide a measure of vicarious experience and insight into the black person's despair and frustration in today's society. Whether it's from the sometimes brutal pen of James Baldwin, the incisive tongue of Malcolm X, the scholarly prose of a sociologist, or the emotion-packed statements of a black minister, the white man in general doesn't fare too well, and the white evangelical comes out even worse, because he should know better.

The Rev. Michael Haynes, black minister at the Twelfth Baptist Church in Boston, and a representative in the Massachusetts Legislature, gave this account in an address at Park Street Church in Boston:

> My entire lifetime was spent just a few yards from a great evangelical church. I had lived two-thirds of my life before I ever received an invitation to come in. As a child whose family had just moved into a fast-changing white neighborhood on the edge of a Negro ghetto, I sat on the stairs of this church and played. I looked into the downstairs window as white face upon white face sat around tables at church suppers. I can vividly recall one day that I, a poor black child whose

> family was on welfare, yelled into the window of this church, "We're hungry. Give us something to eat!" only to have a beautiful white lady come out and tell my brother and me how rude we were.
>
> Nevertheless, thank God, His love found me. And . . . it was not through the church that I was lifted from the sinking sands of misdirection and degredation. It was through a . . . settlement house that I was lifted high enough to be able to catch a breath of air in this society.[1]

A white church worker was wheeled on a stretcher into a two-bed ward in a hospital in a large city. Sick as she was, she refused to remain in that room because the patient in the other bed was a black woman.

Because this kind of rejection, and far worse, has been the repeated experience of black people for generations, vast numbers of them reject Christianity as the white man's religion, and Christ as the white man's God.

From all the books I read on the subject (and I didn't begin to scratch the surface of what's available), the overriding impression was the intense hostility felt by the black man for the white, a hostility which has been kept under the surface for years, and which was only recently erupted, a hostility which is understandable in light of the hopelessness of the situation.

As James Baldwin wrote in a letter to his

nephew, "You were born where you were born and faced the future that you faced because you were black and for no other reason."[2]

Trapped by color. It made me feel sick inside. Which one of us can predetermine his color or nationality? Yet how ingrained is the prejudice.

Black hostility is an enigma to white people. They can't understand it. They are often under the false impression that the great American dream is available to anyone as long as he works for it.

"My parents came over from the old country. We didn't have a thing. But my dad worked hard, long hours, with little pay, and we made it," we hear people say. And the prevailing assumption is that any black person could do as well if he would just work a little harder. Problem is, he's lazy! Then I heard of the black man who had a master's degree in education and who is working as a janitor because no adequate teaching position was available to him.

And when white people do become aware of racial needs and problems and try to get involved, they often meet with rejection and hostility. And their resulting attitude is, "Well, if that's the way you want it, I'll leave you alone to work out your own problems!"

But I know a white Christian homemaker who lives in the suburbs and started teaching a weekly released-time class at an inner-city church. (Public schools allow children one hour a week for religious instruction in the church of their choice.)

This was the hour Ann drove in to one of the worse city neighborhoods. She admits that she responded to a plea for help and started her work with the attitude, *Here I am to help you!* "Now after three years," she went on, "I am really grasping what it means to extend *myself,* to give myself to the children and parents with whom I work. The Christian has to learn that Christianity is not a comfortable thing. We have to be willing to be spent!"

I phoned Ann one Saturday afternoon. She was in the middle of washing a pile of muddy clothes, and drying sopping gym shoes. She had taken a group of her inner-city students on a picnic. It had rained. And now she was getting them all dried out as any mother would. Ann gives herself, not just her help, to her black friends.

As I thought of this I was reminded of Moses' experience. He went to his oppressed people as a knight in shining armor to "deliver" them. His intentions were so good! He killed an Egyptian to prove his sincerity. And he was met with hostility and rejection from the people he tried to help.

It took forty years of living as a fugitive in the desert, working hard for a living, before Moses was ready to deliver his people. This time he was able to really identify with them. He understood their needs. He could give himself, not just the "help" of a privileged prince in the palace. Most important, he went to the people in the power of God. In the power of God, white Christians can learn to extend themselves to black people and see dramatic results. God still delivers bound people—black or white.

The community in which we live has had a white and black population for over fifty years. When the Lord began making me sensitive to racial issues, I not only read books on the subject, but began to listen to what black people, particularly black Christians, had to say.

One memorable experience in this connection was attending a conference for Christian women on the South Side of Chicago. Of the three-hundred women present, 99 percent were black. Some of the most articulate speakers I have ever heard spoke at that conference. There was a sharp, intense quality to their expressions of personal faith in God which had obviously been honed through years of abrasive experience. They knew God as perhaps I would never know him. They had so much to share. But those who could benefit the most weren't listening and probably never would be.

I came home from that conference deeply stirred, and prayed that the Lord would establish a line of communication across the racial barrier in our own community. How could he do it?

"Through Christians," came the inner response.

"But, Lord, I don't know any black Christians in our community," I replied.

"I do," said the Lord.

Great. The Lord knew who the Christians were,

but I didn't. How could I get to know the Christians in my own community? I prayed again, "OK, Lord, you know the Christians in this community. In some way please give me one black Christian friend."

It was only about two weeks later that a women's missionary conference was held at our church. I was so tired that I nearly didn't go, but I felt I had to. As soon as I reached the church I knew the reason for the inner compulsion. In the sea of white faces were three black ones. As soon as the afternoon session was over, I fairly pounced on these ladies. It took only a few minutes to discover that they were neighbors, women from the community. The Lord hadn't brought one, but three.

Since that day, a firm friendship has developed. These women started attending one of our neighborhood Bible studies. They brought others into the group. We meet in one another's homes. We pray together about our family and community needs. We share our problems. One of the black ladies teaches a child-evangelism class in her home. Our seven-year-old daughter has had the benefit of her teaching all year. And one of the women in the Bible study (who happens to be white) works with her.

The accepted fact in our community is that little love is lost between whites and Negroes. But in the Bible-study group there is a bond of love and mutual respect between the white and black women. We couldn't have engineered such unity. The Lord did it, and it's beautiful!

"For Christ Himself is our way of peace. He has made peace between us . . . by making us all one family, breaking down the wall of contempt [or hostility] that used to separate us. By his death He ended the angry resentment between us."[3] No true Christian, white or black, can come to the cross of Jesus Christ and view the God-Man pouring out his life for all men, and then turn away to justify the bitterness and resentment in his own heart for a person of a different color. In Christ Jesus we are *one*, and the Bible means just that. If barriers still exist, they have been built by man, not by God.

What can concerned Christians do about racial issues? Read. Yes, and listen, and learn. Pray for a change of attitude. Then let Christians find each other. Pray for a Christian friend outside your own ethnic circle, and develop a friendship. Extend yourself. Trust the Lord.

White Christians also need to feel with black Christians and pray fervently for them. They are part of the body of Christ and if the whole body doesn't hurt when part of it is hurting so badly, then there's something wrong with the body.

And white Christians should support and encourage black ministers who declare the Word of God in truth. Let them preach in white pulpits. We had a lovely black Christian woman speak at a Bible-study conference recently, and it was an enriching experience for all of us. One of her statements was, "Unity depends on a love relationship among people." But before a love relationship can develop, people have to get to know each other. And she suggested that one way for people in a community to get acquainted is for two churches to exchange names of their members. Each person in one church would draw the name of a member in another church. During the week he would phone that person and share with him a verse of Scripture, and also ask for any prayer requests.

The same sort of exchange could take place on a teen-age level. Instead of black and white adults exchanging verbal barbs, and black and white young people exchanging blows in a tense high school, they would be sharing the Word of God together and praying for each other. It wouldn't have to be limited to black and white, but could be between Catholic and Protestant, or Protestant and Protestant. It just might revolutionize a community!

When we talk of friendship and broken barriers, there is lurking in the back of most people's minds the invariable question of interracial marriage. How far are we expected to go on this friendship bit? This is a major problem for many people. I think every Christian parent wants to see his child happily married. The one injunction the Bible seems to clear give is that believers in Jesus Christ should not marry nonbelievers. The Bible also says that the human race is of "one blood." This apparently leaves the rest of the field rather wide open.

But it's a mistake for white people to think that black people are waiting in line to marry whites. They aren't! It is also a mistake for a white person to marry a black just to show how "liberated" he is. Rebellion against parents or society or any established order of things provides a very shaky foundation for marriage, and marriage between any two people demands far more than mere color evaluation.

A white Christian girl fell deeply in love with a black Christian man she met at a church she attended. Godly black Christians in that church discerned that the man was a phony, and rescued the girl from what could have been a disastrous marriage. It wasn't basically a question of black and white. In this case, it was a question of character.

Psychological difficulties related to color are not the exclusive problems of whites either. For example: a light-skinned black woman married a white man. They had a son who looked like the father and a daughter who was much darker than the mother. The mother had a built-in hang-up on color and she hated her dark-skinned daughter. She totally rejected her. The daughter married a black man from Africa and went to live there. But that marriage ended in divorce because the Western-oriented black woman could not adjust to the African culture of her black husband. For every marriage, there is far more to be considered than color alone. An interracial couple in our society would have to be strong enough to personally withstand, and also to help their children resist the pressures of a society which is basically hostile to such a union. Each Christian person contemplating marriage needs to seek the mind and will of God. I have seen interracial marriages which have worked well when the husband and wife have had a firm faith in God and a strong love for each other. But aren't these the essential ingredients for *every* good marriage?

The best of intentions can be misunderstood. A white Christian teen-ager had worked diligently to make friends of black kids in her high school. One afternoon a black boy drowned in a nearby lake. It happened so fast that none of his white buddies could get to him soon enough to save him. All the young people, black and white, who were swimming at the time, developed cramps. But the black boy went under and didn't come up again.

In school the next morning, when the white girl heard of the tragedy, she wept. A black girl bitterly questioned her, "Why are you crying? You're white! You're one of the murderers!" The black kids blamed the white ones for not saving the drowning boy. It was unreasonable resentment. However, the operating principles for Christians do not alter just because there are difficulties or irrationality.

The white Christian girl reestablished communication with her black friends. She and many other white students attended the funeral and heard the dead boy's father declare, "I know where my son is today because he knew Jesus Christ as his Lord and Savior. He was ready to die!" The tragedy ended with a church full of young people of both races who felt the compelling unity and optimism which come with faith in Christ.

Christ said we were to love one another, and he didn't make it conditional on whether we were loved in return. A beautiful example of this principle in operation was exhibited by Mrs. Taylor, a teacher in the Southwest.

Mrs. Taylor was ready to retire from teaching when the Lord pushed her into involvement with operation Head Start. And so she went for six weeks' training in the Head Start program. I'm going to let Mrs. Taylor pick up the story at that point:

"My dormitory roommate arrived eight hours after I had settled myself in the room. The college girl at the desk hit the panic button.

" 'She's a Negro! *Will* you share the room with her?'

"I suggested she ask the black woman if *she* would share the room with *me*!

"That left us both in agreement to live in the same room for six weeks. After faithfully doing all the room cleaning alone for four weeks, I learned that my roommate was telling friends that her ultimate desire had been reached—she had a white maid! It was an easy blessing to give her. There wasn't much work to it, and I needed the exercise! Also, I had prayed before coming, 'Let peace on earth begin with mc.' Gradually, a friendship developed. She began giving help with the chores. And we still keep in touch with warm friendly letters."

Mrs. Taylor could so easily have let her pride get in the way of this developing friendship. Our normal reaction is to deal snub for snub, word for word, blow for blow.

The Bible gives the only formula that really works: "Never pay back evil for evil. Conquer evil by *doing good.*"[4]

politics and principles

Harry Strom, premier of Alberta, Canada, made this statement:

> "I have never considered my Christianity a handicap in any way in political service. In political life, God often uses previous experiences as stepping-stones to holding office. I would give this advice to young people: continue in day-by-day devotion to Christ. God rewards faithfulness to the tasks we face each day, regardless of what might come in the future."

Beyond voting, writing an occasional letter to an elected official, and getting emotionally involved in local issues, my own knowledge of politics was very slim. So, I decided I needed to observe and learn.

"There is no such thing as an honest politician!" is the frequently heard adage. Politics is considered a dirty game, and most people seem to accept it that way. It is assumed that all the glowing promises given by a political candidate will be broken or forgotten once that candidate is in office. The opposition will keep reminding him of unfulfilled pledges, but the average voter tends to write it all off as part of the game of "playing politics."

This generally accepted frame of reference for the political arena is diametrically opposed to the basic tenets of Christianity. Consequently, many Christians deliberately avoid involvement in politics. Some very sincere Christians I know feel that all forms of government are so much a part of a godless world system that they won't even vote. They feel that since a Christian's citizenship is in heaven, he shouldn't get too committed to an earthly citizenship. I respect their feelings in this.

However, the Bible tells of all kinds of people—God-fearing people—who became involved in varying levels of the government under which they lived. The Lord established government to preserve order in society. It came as quite a shock to one of the ladies in our Bible-study group when she discovered that God's form of government was not a democracy! It was a theocracy. In the Old Testament God was king. He made the laws. He set up rulers. He declared war. He made peace. He took care of health and welfare. He kept tight control over crime. He established capital punishment.

There were no penitentiaries, but for certain crimes the convicted person was restricted to certain cities for a period of time. God cared for property rights, the poor, justice, management and labor, education, and religion. He was even interested in conservation of natural resources. God's blueprint for government and society is laid out in the first five books of the Bible.

When the people acknowledged God's leadership and lived according to his plans, they found they had a well-ordered society. God maintained a careful balance between the importance of the individual and the importance of society as a whole.

Man, independent creature that he is, kept thinking he could improve on God. He resented the restrictive nature of God's laws. He didn't like the absolute monarchy of theocracy. He wanted to do his own thing in his own way and, whenever he did it, chaos and anarchy resulted. Things would get so out of hand that in desperation the people would cry to God for help. With God back in control, things went much better. But in prosperity and peace the people once again forgot God and it was back to violence and chaos and injustice.

Throughout the Bible, people lived under all kinds of governmental systems–judges, monarchies, foreign oppressors. When Jesus Christ entered human history, the Jewish people were a captive nation under Roman rule. They paid heavy taxes to a foreign power. Both the political and religious establishments were corrupt.

Jesus' followers would gladly have seen their leader overthrow the hated Roman Empire and its rotten internal system of government and set up his own kingdom with himself as king. But violent revolution was not his intent. Jesus established a kingdom which transcended the political system of his day, and which transcends systems of government in every generation. Jesus was a good citizen. He paid his taxes. He obeyed the laws. He exposed corruption, but he threatened no one's life. He sensitized consciences wherever he went. Changes followed in his wake. And he did this without carrying a gun, threatening people, or even wielding the power of the ballot box. In producing change, he never compromised his integrity. He always did what was right.

One day he spotted one of the top tax collectors. The man was a crook. He had used his position to extort money from helpless taxpayers. He was rich. Jesus looked at this man and *didn't* say, "I'm going to sue you for every cent you've robbed from innocent people!" Nor did he say, "You're such a crook, you belong in jail!" Nor, "Shoot the man! He doesn't deserve to live!" Instead, he said, "You'd better hurry home, because I'm coming to your house for dinner!" To some, his action seemed to condone the man's illegal activities.

But something significant was transpiring in that tax collector's house. Face to face with Jesus Christ, the tax collector developed a terrifically guilty conscience. He decided his wealth wasn't worth the price on his own soul. He invited Christ into his home and into his life. A dramatic change for the better took place. Half of his wealth he gave to the poor. And everyone he had cheated he repaid, with interest. The change in him produced social action as well as moral responsibility.

Jesus changed the rotten system by changing people. A system can never be changed for the better unless people are changed. The greatest dynamic for producing change is love. Christians should exhibit the love of Christ on all levels of political involvement, whether it's in the PTA, or the local, state, or national government.

A Christian should never compromise his integrity. He should always do what is right. A local PTA had a routine election of officers recently. Usually the slate of officers presented by the nominating committee is accepted as given because it's so hard to get anyone willing to work. However, for some reason best known to the participants, a pressure group had come with an alternate slate, and had packed the meeting with enough of their backers to win quite handily. There was nothing wrong with their nominees for office. They were very nice, fine people. It was all proper and legal except for one point. The PTA has a rule that a person must be a member for thirty days before being qualified to vote. However, quite a few people came who were not members. That night they applied for membership, paid their dues, and asked for a ballot. When reminded of the rule for voting, the reply was, "If you won't let us vote, we'll expose such and such." And the threat was to bring to light a technical illegality on the other side of the fence. The new members were permitted to vote.

A few weeks later a similar situation developed, only this time a whole township was involved and the decision would affect approximately 75,000 people. The harassment was even heavier. I knew of at least one threatening phone call as the day for the crucial vote drew near. Both sides tried to apply pressure, but the group exerting the highest amount of pressure, and who had the majority vote, won the day.

How does a Christian live in a system like this and respond to it? First, he has the responsibility of being as well informed as possible on candidates and issues before voting. After he has carefully considered the issues, voted (on the bases of character and qualifications rather than charisma), then he should quietly accept the outcome and *pray* for the people who were put into the positions of authority.

There's an interesting verse in the book of Proverbs which says, "The lot is cast into the lap, but the decision is wholly from the *Lord*."[1] The prophet Daniel said, "The Most High overrules the kingdoms of men, and He appoints anyone He desires to reign over them"[2] The apostle Paul expressed it in these terms: "There is no government anywhere that God has not placed in power."[3]

These statements should encourage Christians. God has the final say in any government, local or national. All who are in authority have been placed in those positions by the Lord himself. He never loses control over the affairs of men. His people, knowing this, need not lose their cool.

Furthermore, the best way to expose the corrupt and the evil is to be committed to doing what is right and just and true. The apostle Paul in his letter to the Ephesians wrote that we should expose evildoing by the light, for "when anything is exposed by the light it becomes visible."[4]

Even Elijah Muhammad, leader of the Black Muslims, propounds this principle. One day while instructing Malcom X, Mr. Muhammad put a clean glass of water on a table next to a dirty glass of water. Then he turned to Malcolm X and asked, " 'You want to know how to spread my teachings?' and he pointed to the glasses of water. 'Don't condemn if you see a person has a dirty glass of water,' he said, 'just show them the clean glass of water that you have. When they inspect it, you won't have to say that yours is better.' "[5]

A Christian turns on the light, full force. And the light exposes darkness. What is our light? Christ. If every believer truly lived Christ in every aspect of his life the hidden works of darkness would be exposed to full view.

One Christian family suffered wind damage to their roof. The insurance adjuster came and said,

"Well, you have about $50 worth of damage, but I can make a claim for you to get a whole new roof."

"Thanks," replied the householder, "we need a new roof, but we're only interested in claiming the amount of the damage."

"You're crazy," was the man's retort. "Everyone else does it!"

It is much easier to decry dishonesty in someone else than to *be* honest in everything myself, especially the kind of honesty and integrity that no one else knows about.

It is much easier to cry "apostate" than to live by the principles of the Word of God myself.

It is much easier to hate a hater than to *love* that hater.

It is much easier to accuse someone else of injustice than to be just in all my thinking and actions.

It is much easier to demand *my* rights than to give someone else his.

It is much easier to call someone else a gossip than to control my own slanderous tongue. In a climate when suspicion and fear run so high, a Christian needs to be extra careful not to contribute to the health and welfare of unfounded rumors. The other day a fire started in a neighbor's garage. The first report was that it was caused by the careless smoking on the part of some young people. Before the telephones had a chance to warm up, the story had expanded to "teen-agers smoking marijuana." The marijuana angle later proved untrue, as did *any* kind of smoking. It was uncertain how the fire started.

A minister in a large Eastern city which has a long history of domination by machine politics, believes that Christians should be heard in every level of the community—in the PTA, the town council, as aldermen, etc.

"But first," he said, "the Christian must *earn* the right to be heard. He must be as dedicated a Christian in politics as we expect every missionary or minister to be in his field. Christians need to learn to move in all kinds of environments and remain people of impeccable integrity."

This man is not a politician, but he moves among politicians with ease, and even the mayor's office is open to him. He has made himself available. He will sit in a bar and sip ginger ale while listening to the problems which the police captain pours out as he drinks his beer. He goes to the firehouse and just talks with firemen when they have no calls. As a result, firemen and police sergeants and politicans have come to him with their marital troubles or asked him to pray with them when their own children have gotten hooked on drugs. In all his associations he has never sacrificed his integrity; he speaks out on issues, he points people to Jesus Christ, and he conducts about thirteen Bible studies a week. People from the mayor on down listen.

As evangelicals we have the duty to examine

> political issues of our day in the light of Scripture—not only such typically evangelical concerns as to whether liquor will be sold on Sunday, but the basic issues of political life such as: What is the task of the state? What should be our Christian attitude toward the welfare state? What should we think of such matters as state aid to independent schools? Must we support the state in every war or are there limits of support?[6]

Besides being knowledgeable on issues, is it possible to actually be involved in politics and remain untainted?

"I had myself almost convinced that it was impossible," said Dr. E., a school business administrator with an impressive list of credentials in education who was contemplating running for political office. "Well-meaning Christians told me the political game was dirty, and you had to play dirty to win," he went on: "Then I realized that getting into office wouldn't suddenly make me honest if I hadn't been honest on the way up. We need to stop deceiving ourselves and be committed to truth. I have to face and honestly admit to the disparities in my own life before I can put my finger on them in the community. There is such a wide gap between what we *say* and what we *do*. For example, in the city in which I'm interested we say, 'In our schools the children come first.' But in practice the children actually come last. It's the teachers and principals who come first. They choose where they want to teach. The parents as taxpayers exert an influence to some degree on education. The best interest of the children in the whole community is the last consideration given. The Christian cannot be silent when he sees wrongs, but he must begin with the wrongs in himself."

The Bible tells of a number of people who reached top positions in government–Daniel, Mordecai, and Joseph were three. They all exhibited courage and integrity on the way up and eventually wielded great influence and power in their countries.

Joseph, as a slave, didn't play politics to win favors with those in power. The greatest test of his integrity came behind closed doors. He could have played the game of seduction and influence to the fullest advantage of political expediency. But he had already submitted to the authority of God in his life, and his personal relationship with God wouldn't permit him to bow to this secret pressure.

The Christ-dominated life exhibits the same high degree of integrity behind closed doors, when no one is looking, as it does in full public view. For Joseph, maintaining his integrity was of greater importance than getting out of a tight situation through expediency. As a result he was framed and thrown in jail. But it was a man with this high caliber of character that Egypt needed to conduct the welfare program for the nation. Joseph didn't squander the profits during the years of prosperity, and he wasn't subject to political patronage nor partisanship when an equal distribution of food was essential to all people. He didn't even withhold food out of bitterness and resentment toward those who had wronged him.

When his brothers traveled to Egypt for food, he could so easily have said, "Now's my chance to get even. Let them starve!" Again, his personal relationship with God wouldn't allow him to do that.

This principle, if it had been more widely known and practiced, might have helped in a recent vote in our area. Several years ago a nearby township voted to build a junior college. An adjoining township was invited to share in the project but decided against participation. The school was built, the taxes went up, and the junior college program became a healthy one with a fine reputation. And now the neighboring township wants in.

"Nuts to them!" is the bitter sentiment of many of the local residents. "Where were they when we needed them? Now that we have a success going, they want to be included."

The referendum was voted down by a large margin. It is apparent that the bitter antagonism of seven years' past has neither been forgiven nor forgotten.

Joseph didn't harbor that kind of spite against his brothers. He said to them, "You meant evil against me; but God meant it for good, to bring it about that many people should be kept alive, as they are today."[7] Perhaps this kind of action is "poor politics," but it's great Christianity! And these are principles which function not only in government but in every area of life.

I know of a fine Christian woman who sought and gained the office of building inspector in her town. And there are other Christians who are on school boards, in town councils, or serving as state representatives, aldermen, and in other elected positions at a "grass roots" level. Hopefully, they have taken a dynamic Christianity into their positions. We need many more of them.

Many people feel that the key to solutions of urban problems, in particular, is through politics. Dr. E. is interested in the political field of a large city:

"I have decided that to run for office in this city, I would have to do it as an independent," he said. "Both political parties exert too much pressure to play *their* game *their* way and, as a Christian, I would rather avoid the associations that either party would bring."

"How could you muster the support you would need for such a large undertaking?" I asked him.

"Well, it would take manpower, of course. Lots of volunteer manpower. I would like to use hundreds of Christian young people to distribute promotional material in every precinct in the city. I would also use them as poll-watchers on election day. The other big thing is—money. Politics is an expensive game. The cost of advertising and communications is very high. Evangelicals are very slow to give to political ventures. For one thing, there are no income-tax deductions granted for political contributions. Consequently, it is often the liberal with a humanitarian view who will invest all kinds of money to get his man in. Christians are willing to help with the cause of Christ indirectly as long as someone else pays for it. But it is money and people which 'win' in politics. You need both."

Congressman John B. Anderson, a representative from the state of Illinois and an outstanding Christian politician, made this statement:

> We need to find a way in which individual Christians in the churches can be encouraged to make individual contributions to the political process. . . . It makes more sense to talk about infusing the political system with new energy, ideas, and commitment from the bottom up than from the top down.[8]

Congressman Anderson also makes this pertinent comment:

> We must also remember that it is not necessary for Christians to agree on political questions to be effective as Christians in the political order. . . . We must be careful not to substitute political unity for spiritual unity as a criterion of Christian fellowship.[9]

This is the area in which I believe Paul's injunction to "walk in love" is particularly relevant. We live in a day of political extremes from the "far right" to the "far left" and all stages in between. And in most categories from one end to the other there are Christians.

The yardstick we use for measuring our walk of love is Christ's love. He gave himself not only for people who loved him, but also for those who hated and despised him. The Christian walks in love toward all men—his fellow believer with whom he may not agree, those whose political philosophies are extreme or moderate. In various areas of politics the Christian can show his love through service. Because Christ's love motivates him, he will not make decisions purely in response to power groups seeking to protect vested interests (somehow I cannot picture Joseph yielding to the powerful lobbies with the most money), he will work for the benefit of all people—regardless of race or religion, he won't allow stronger groups to manipulate or exploit the weak or ignorant, he won't consider profit more important than people.

Finally, as Senator Mark Hatfield has said,

> We must always remember that regardless of the circumstances the world is in, history remains under God's sovereignty. In Ephesians, Paul writes that God "purposes in his sovereign will that all human history shall be consummated in Christ, that everything that exists in Heaven or earth shall find its perfection and fulfillment in Him."[10]

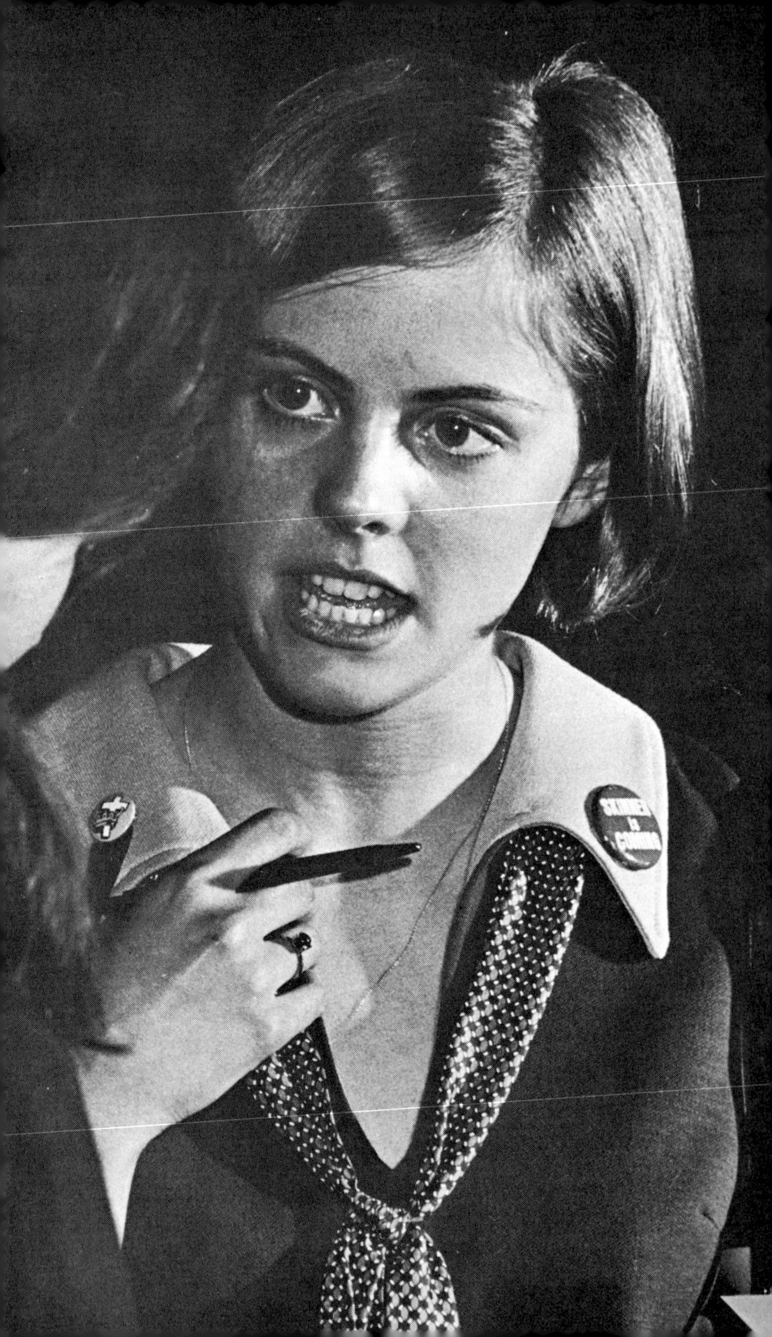
SKINNER
is
COMING

the youth explosion

Two plus two equals four. It always has. It always will. There's security in that. Mathematics is exact. Cause and effect. Logic. This plus this *has* to equal that. Even children apply this kind of logic to certain causes and effects:

"The sun's coming out!" wailed our seven-year-old one day in early spring.

"That's great," I replied. "It's been a long, gray winter."

"No, it's not great!" she continued emphatically, "'cause it means spring and summer are coming and so are all the teen-agers!"

For her, spring heralded not just tulips and grass, but large groups of teen-agers congregating on the school grounds across the street from our house with their motorcycles, souped-up cars, transistor radios, and beer cans. To a first grader they are a formidable force too large to cope with. But warm weather brings out teen-agers as surely as contact with poison ivy produces a rash! And to our daughter, they're about as welcome!

We like to be able to put things in convenient pigeonholes. This cause will produce that effect and it will not vary. "If you put this and this into a marriage, then it's bound to be a happy one." Or, "If you raise your child this way, he will turn out to be a responsible adult." We want simplistic formulas so that we can be sure of success. The only problem is that sometimes human nature just doesn't work that way.

Consequently, parents today are facing a generation of young people who just aren't turning out in accordance with their planned expectations. Probably few generations of young people have had the material advantages of the "good life" as this one has. They have benefited from giant strides in medicine and education. Everything should be rosy and beautiful. "Instead, it's a mess" says the distraught parent. "Kids are screaming, throwing rocks, closing down institutions, starting fires, growing long hair, smoking pot, marching, burning draft cards, running away from gorgeous homes. Why?"

"It's Dr. Spock's fault! He encouraged parents to be too permissive," someone answers.

"It's all part of a 'commie' plot," is another's reply.

"If these children had been given the proper

spiritual training from the time they were two years of age, this would never have happened!" is someone else's dogmatic declaration.

"Right," another person adds. "The Bible says, 'Train up a child in the way he should go, and when he is old, he will not depart from it.' "[1]

Discipline produces order, patriotism—good citizens; church attendance—moral people; spiritual input—spiritual results; the right causes—the proper effects; and if it doesn't work that way then it has to be the fault of Dr. Spock, Communists, or poor parents. It's just that simple!

"But it isn't that simple," cries a brokenhearted Christian mother. "We did all the right things. We have always taken our children to church and Sunday school. We didn't 'send' them. Our home was filled with both love and firm discipline. We're good citizens. We have taught our children spiritual truths and moral principles in our home. I never dreamed that one of *my* daughters could end up on dope and alcohol, but she did! Her personality changed. Life became unbearable for all of us. The minute she hit eighteen she left to live on her own. I must admit the atmosphere improved for the rest of the family when she went. But I keep asking, 'Why? Why?' It just shouldn't have turned out that way."

And more and more Christian parents are asking the same thing. The casualty rate in good Christian homes seems to be rising steadily. There is the young nineteen-year-old who was born into a "straight, straight" Christian family. He learned John 3:16. He asked God into his heart at the age of seven. "Everyone was happy and I felt cool," he said.

He was all that a "nice Christian boy" should be until he went to college. But the pressures of wrong associations started him on marijuana, then LSD, and finally heroin. He had himself persuaded that he could actually be a better witness to "acid heads" about God by being one himself. Instead, he blew his mind and discovered that God wasn't real to him at all. He had no peace, "I didn't know who I was, or even if I was–I really freaked out!" He tried to discover himself through dope, but he got no answers.

People whose children have been absorbed into society and are considered "acceptable" tend to have pat answers to these problems. Those whose children have made a departure from the so-called "norm" have few answers, especially when they have sincerely sought, with the Lord's help, to be good parents.

But what is actually "acceptable" or "normal" or "successful"? Is the person who never clashes with society "acceptable"? Is the person who is satisfied with the status quo the "norm"? Is the person with a healthy bank account, nice home in the suburbs, two cars, and color TV a "success"?

"I grew up in the suburbs," a college senior told me. "Clothes, vacations, fame are big goals for a young person, but they're not enough. A lot of young people are turned off on 'success' because they have lived close to successful people. The criterion for judging a 'good family' has been if they are churchgoers, if their kids get good grades and are athletic. And I don't think that's a valid basis for judgment."

"What do you think is a valid basis for judgment?" I asked.

"I think 'success' in a family is determined by interpersonal relationships. Is there harmony in the home when no one else is around? Are the parents geared to producing spiritually mature families?"

Here was a young man who objected to the Christianity he had seen while he was growing up because it was mechanical. People went through the motions. But it was all so hollow. Is this a valid criticism? How many of the spiritual motions do we go through because that's what is expected, rather than because we're motivated by genuine love for Jesus Christ?

Young people look for the real and the genuine. They are also highly critical—and always have been. Seldom do they admit that something is all right. It can always be improved *their* way. And in defense of Christians who go through certain "motions" and follow certain traditions, perhaps to them these practices have great meaning and are an expression of true faith. They may seem mechanical to the young person because he himself has not had a vital experience of faith with God.

Nevertheless young people today are thinking through the traditions of their churches and of society. And they are deeply disturbed. Many young voices are genuinely pleading for compassion and an equitable justice in society.

One young person is concerned about her church. There doesn't seem to be unity. There are "social levels." She would like to say something, but "it wouldn't do any good, anyway. Nobody would listen."

There's often a great sense of despair and hopelessness. Young people don't want to be forced into a mold set for them by "the Establishment." But what mold do they fit? There must be more to life than going to college just because my parents went, or the endless routine of getting up in the morning, going to work, coming home, watching TV, and going to bed. Surely a person must have more meaning to life than this. There's a quest for personal identity.

"Do your own thing" is the cry of the day, but how do I do my own thing if I don't know who I am?

The crisis of identity is as old as man himself. The teen-agers in the Bible who made an impact in their generations, knew who they were, what their purpose in life was, and *accepted* themselves and their lot in life. Why? Because each of them was personally related to God.

Samuel was very young when he was sent away from home for his religious training. The comment made of him was; "Samuel was ministering to the *Lord* under Eli,"[2] Eli, although a priest, represented a corrupt establishment. Yet Samuel accepted his position under him because he was rightly related to God and was serving the Lord, not Eli. And when Samuel talked to Eli, Eli listened. There was no "generation gap."

The slave girl who was captured by the Syrian army was separated from her family by force and became a servant to Naaman's wife. She accepted this tremendous tragedy in her life without bitterness, and communicated to her enemy captor a message of hope that saved his life. Why? Because she was rightly related to the living God of Israel. And when this young girl said something, the commander of the Syrian army listened and acted on what she said. There was no "generation gap."

Daniel and his friends were teen-agers when they were uprooted from their homes and trained for special service in the king's court. They courageously stood for what they believed. And they were ready to accept the consequences for their action. As a result, the man in charge of them listened to them, and eventually the king listened too. Why? Because they had a personal faith relationship with the Lord and knew what *he* expected of them, and they accepted this.

"When a man's ways please the *Lord,* he makes even his enemies to be at peace with him."[3]

Jesus knew who he was and his mission in life by the time he was twelve. Granted, he was an exceptional child. But even at the point when he recognized that he was the Son of God and that he was to do his Father's work, he willingly went home and submitted himself to the authority of his earthly parents, though he was probably the only child who ever lived who could truly say, "I know more than my parents!" Furthermore, he grew up in a town not known for anything spectacular. It was just an ordinary town with ordinary people who spoke with countrified accents!

Jesus didn't try to explain his humble upbringing. He didn't ask people to understand him, but he asked them to accept him. He accepted himself. He accepted his way of life.

Each person's life is unique. It is not intended to exactly duplicate someone else's. Each set of circumstances is different. I can moan and complain about my life, but it I do, I am actually saying, "God has cheated me, and I resent it!" Or, I can accept my life as it is and look for ways to use to the best advantage all the circumstances which are uniquely mine.

This puts the ghetto child and the affluent suburbanite on the same level. Each is unique. Tom Skinner has frequently said, "The ghetto child is not culturally deprived. He is culturally rich. His culture is just not the same. The ghetto child has a high degree of 'copability.' " He learns early to cope with life as he finds it.

We have artificial labels to put on things—"better" or "worse." If I truly accept myself as I am, I am more capable of accepting someone else as he is. God accepts me when I come to him in simple faith. In response to this faith Christ makes me a new person. I can then look at myself honestly and objectively and, in his power, accept what he made me and the plan he has for me.

This is essentially the operating philosophy of a Christian education center in a black community in one of the suburbs. The primary goal of the center is "to win children to Jesus Christ through teaching them about the black culture as it is found in the Word of God," said the enthusiastic director. "We have to let black children know that they have a part in God's plan. They are important to God. We try to teach children to be proud of themselves. And when they let Christ live in them, he makes them truly free."

Another very dynamic Christian woman is having a similar outreach with gangs. She speaks in areas that are considered dangerous. One night a very tough-looking gang of fellows and girls invaded her meeting. They danced up the aisles and tried to break up the service. Miss E. just had everyone stand and quietly pray. Gradually the gang quieted down and backed off. They were impressed. Miss E. made a point of meeting the gang leader that night and invited him to her next meeting. She said to him, "Your life came from God. You were made in the image of God, not to live like an animal, but like a man, with dignity. But you need to be changed."

The gang leader and his gang showed up again. They listened. Then the leader asked if he could say something, "We have never had anyone come to talk to us. We don't know how to live. Church members walk past us acting like they are better than us. We didn't know how to act here. We don't have Bibles. If we go to church, we are ushered out. We aren't wanted!"

But Miss E. warmly conveys her belief that everyone has worth. As a result some gang members have trusted Jesus Christ. One fellow who pushed dope and knifed people accepted Christ, and he said, "Something really happened to me. All the hate left. I love everybody!" Another said, "It feels so good to be clean!"

The director of a rescue mission told me of a new concept in camp programming which they were initiating. "It's called 'Carload Camping,'" he said.

"We deal with children who have no sense of individual worth. The mission is training adults to take these children in their cars, rather than the entire group together on a bus. In a car with a smaller group of children, the adults can relate to them as individuals. At camp the adults will remain involved with the same children as 'substitute parents.' The camp program will be unstructured. The emphasis will be on personal involvement and love. The teaching will be done informally as the 'family' walks through the woods, or as the occasion gives rise to it."

A Christian second-grade teacher faced a severe "identity crisis" among her pupils. Half her class didn't know who their fathers were. They didn't have the security of family identification. Her approach was to introduce her children to Christ. "When they receive him, then they are members of God's family. God is their father. And they can be proud of their family."

A police officer who works as a counselor in a public high school says that often his role is that of a substitute father.

Perhaps the most touching story I heard in this connection was about a Christian nurse who left the position of director of nurses in a suburban hospital to teach nursing in a vocational school in the inner city. "What do you think *you* can give to these children?" someone challenged. "You don't speak their language!"

"It is true. I don't talk their language," Mrs. J. said. "But I do have something to give. I have values to transmit. I'm not going to change my language, but I'll share myself."

Before long, communication in both directions was wide open in her class of sixteen-year-old girls. "I looked for ways to praise them. I would say, 'My, you did that well. Now try this and see how well you do.' "

As she moved around the room, instructing, conversing, encouraging, the girls began to open up. She discovered three of them had babies at home and three more were pregnant.

"They were really ignorant of what life was all about," Mrs. Jr. said. "So then I began to talk to them about the God-given graces of womanhood. In the framework of biblical principles, I told them they could be proud of being women, they could have pride in their femininity, they could have pride in their service in hospitals. But their womanhood was to be cherished, as a gift from God, not to be abused." She instilled in these young girls a feeling of self-worth, of purpose, of meaning to life.

How many of us would have passed them off as cheap tramps? Mrs. J. considered those girls her special mission field. She loved them. And they responded. Besides that, she trained them so well professionally that not one of her "graduates" was turned down when she applied for a job as a nurse's aide.

Christian adults need to listen to young people, no matter how radical their ideas may seem.

One mother of five, three of whom are teenagers, said, "My daughters and I may have been cross with each other all day, but at night they always say, 'Come on, Mom, let's talk,' and we do—about everything. They know they can trust me not to share their confidences with anyone. There are things I don't tell even their father. The girls are fifteen and sixteen now. I hope this line of communication stays open."

It also takes time to be a "good" parent. A young priest said that the biggest social issue he felt his parish faced was for families to get their own "ships in shape."

"We caught a group of seventh graders climbing all over the roof of our church one Saturday at midnight," he said. "When we phoned their homes, the parents weren't there. They were out and had no idea where their kids were. Furthermore, a lot of the parents didn't seem to care. We had to keep those kids in jail for the night until their parents finally showed up."

Do you really know the kinds of problems and pressures your children face in school? Are you listening? Are you there when they need you?

We had a Sunday school parent-teacher evening to which some of the Sunday school young people were invited to inform the adults on the sort of things they faced in their high schools.

One high school senior said, "It's the hippies who bring the reforms in our school. Things that really need to be changed get changed through their efforts."

Another said, "There are more kids on drugs than you can imagine. It's openly available in washrooms, even in the halls of the school."

A sophomore in an integrated high school said, "The black kids who are friendly to whites are called 'oreo cookies' by other blacks. They say they're black on the outside, but white insidc. This is hard pressure for black Christian kids who want to be accepted by their peers."

As the young people talked they communicated

not only the problems, but a real desire to share Christ with their friends in these situations.

A Christian high school counselor said, "Many of the kids I see on drugs are looking for peace. They face so much tension and unrest in their homes that they look for a way out. They don't see their parents facing up to problems and solving them. Their parents move when the issues get too knotty in a community, or escape to Caribbean vacations and leave the kids on their own. Their parents drink or split up when pressures build. It's easier for a father to beat a child than to sit down and work through to the roots of his child's problems and then look for solutions. And I believe," the counselor went on, "that unless a parent involves God in the whole family's life, he isn't going to find any workable solutions."

A Christian juvenile-probation officer said that most of the problems he deals with in young people can be traced back to their homes. The pressures of school and friends are hard on young people, but they are even greater in the homes where parents have yielded to the pressures of society in their lives—the pressures of materialism, of where we spend our time and energies and money. He asked parents, "What kind of standards are you promoting at home? What are your goals? What are you stressing? What kind of husband-wife relationship do you have? As a husband and wife, what is your relationship to God? What place does the Bible have in your lives? Do you forgive? Do your actions and words really reflect Christian love?"

Young people have tremendous pressures put on them. We get disturbed when they yield to these pressures. Perhaps we should be more disturbed by our own yielding to society's more subtle pressures in our lives. It's a real danger, because Paul warned, "Don't let the world around you squeeze you into its own mold, but let God remold your minds from within, so that you may prove in practice that the plan of God for you is good, meets all his demands and moves toward the goal of true maturity."[4]

I believe, too, that the church needs to have a greater communal sense of responsibility for all its young people. Instead of criticizing someone else's children, let's look for opportunities to show an interest and loving concern for these children. Very often young people will be far more responsive to another adult than to their own parents.

I talked to a lady recently who has taken into her home a college-age girl from a Christian home who is on drugs. "You can't imagine the criticism I have gotten from other church people for doing this," she commented.

Other families have done the same thing for young people who have become alienated from their parents and local churches. In some instances the parents have strongly resisted the efforts of other Christians to help their children because they felt it was pointing up their own failure as parents. This is no time for pride to get in the way of God's working. We should thank the Lord for every person who cares enough to make a positive contribution to our sons or daughters.

An elderly lady in our church prays for every single family in the church by name every single day. "And I pray for all the young people twice a day," she said, "because I feel their problems are so great." Because she prays for them so faithfully, she says she finds it's a lot easier to talk to them when she sees them. No communication gap here. She cares, and they know it.

"If I don't talk to somebody, I'm going to absolutely explode!" was the vehement exclamation of one young person. "Please, can we just talk?"

"Sure," I replied. "Let's talk!"

And we did. About six young people, disturbed and somewhat frightened over incidents they had observed in other young people, participated. After they spent about half an hour unloading all their observations, which touched on drug abuse, sex, obscenities, plus their own frustrations, fears and questions related to these things, I asked, "OK, what can we learn from this?" We talked about the "whys" of moral standards. We explored ways of avoiding being enmeshed in the use of drugs ourselves. We discussed the effects of dope, why people use obscenity or rebel against authority. And the discussion led very naturally to the importance of a personal relationship with God to give us the power to live lives that are truly free and not bound by drugs or anything else. They were open and responsive to the application of moral and spiritual principles because someone had been open to their "exploding."

I visited the office of a lovely black Christian lady in her 60's who had felt constrained to become involved in a racially troubled high school. She went at first just to help keep order. But it wasn't long before she had her own office and counseling service. Black and white students found an open and sympathetic ear as well as a wise, gracious counselor. She listened, and so did they. Her office has not only contributed to "keeping the peace," but she has also helped establish communication between students and their parents, students and teachers, students and students. "I start each day with prayer," she said. "I rely upon God to give me the wisdom to find the answers I need for these young people. Many kids seem to have gone mad. They are out of control. I just pray for ways to get their attention. God removes the fear of man from my heart and gives me the proper approach. There is a dire need for people who have the tenacity and will and sincere desire to contribute to a dying world."

We should also encourage the involvement of Christian young people in social issues. A number of Christian adults sponsored young people on a thirty-mile hunger hike to collect money for the underprivileged. Another group of Christian young people is planning a twenty-five-mile march to publicly proclaim their commitment to Christianity. Others are involved in coffee houses, musical groups, and Bible studies on campus.

There is no limit to the ways in which young people can harness their energy for constructive purposes. One group of young people allowed themselves to be hired as "slaves" for a day to paint, wash windows, change storms and screens, do gardening or anything else a homeowner might want done. Another group ran a car wash. The money they earned from these ventures went to special projects.

One of our Christian neighbors sponsored a "block party." A street block was closed off, and she invited a Christian athlete, who was also a musician and known to the local young people, to come with his guitar and provide entertainment. Local young people who had musical groups of their own also were asked to perform. They weren't pros, but they were thrilled with the opportunity to share their interest. She sold soft drinks and popcorn. Adults and teen-agers congregated. They enjoyed each other. It was a great evening. The money collected from the soft drinks and popcorn, as well as a few donations, was used to pay the guest artist, and it was also shared with the amateur musicians.

Our teen-age sons's reaction was, "At last, someone who cared enough to be involved in a positive way."

Some young people, out of a sense of responsibility and concern, are giving their energies to cleaning up highways, creeks and parks, and to picking up trash off streets—not waiting for someone else to do it.

During a recent disturbance on a large university campus, a man in a nice business suit was trying to talk about Christ to the students milling around. Though he was very sincere he was making no headway. Another Christian fellow, looking like a hippie, with long hair, came on the scene. Seeing the man was having trouble, he decided to help him out. He took over the microphone and said, "Look, what this man is saying about Christ is true."

A voice from the back of the crowd challenged, "If your Christianity is true, then give me your sweater. I'm cold back here!"

Without a moment's hesitation, the young man had his sweater off and passed it through the crowd. From that point, he had their complete attention.

The same challenge was thrown at the man in the nice suit, but he disappeared into the crowd.

Yet if those two men came to your church, which one would you be most inclined to welcome? Which one communicated the message of Jesus Christ most effectively? A sure way to lose any audience, but especially an alert young audience, is to fail to back up our preaching with our actions.

Christian parents, Christian adults in a community and church, can contribute a great deal to the welfare of their children and young people by first of all being genuine Christians themselves. Then we still need to do all the "right" things in helping our children to become rightly related to God through personal faith in Christ, taking the time to listen and to care for them, helping them to find their personal identity, their sense of self-worth, their place of contribution in ociety. Having done this, we commit them by faith to the Lord. The choices they make are their own. We still need to accept them and love them even if they don't make the choices we would like them to have made.

Cause and effect. There are so many "causes" which can produce such a variety of "effects." The book of Proverbs is full of them. If you do this, that will be the result. The variable is in the "if." Every person remains an individual with the power of free choice. He has a free will. God has spoken to each of us through his Word. The effect in our lives is in our personal response to him. We can tune in and do as he says, or we can turn him off. The result depends on our choice.

King Solomon told his son that listening to and obeying the Lord is the important thing:

> He who listens to me will dwell secure and will be at ease, without dread of evil. For the LORD gives wisdom; from his mouth come knowledge and understanding. . . . he is a shield to those who walk in integrity, guard-

ing the paths of justice and preserving the way of his saints. Then you will understand righteousness and justice and equity, every good path.[5]

9

"Grandpa's a cool guy"

"It's just too bad people have to live that long," was the unfeeling comment of a nurse as she passed the frail, wrinkled, ninety-two-year-old woman sitting in a wheelchair in the hall of the hospital. No one seemed to need this old lady, nor to want her. She required more time and care than the hospital personnel had to give. Her family wasn't around. So there she sat in a hospital hallway with a blanket tucked around her knees, waiting—for what?

As a student nurse I worked for a while at a state hospital with two large wards for elderly people. Many of the patients didn't belong there. They still had their senses. They were just slow and feeble and their families didn't want the responsibility of caring for them, so they were committed to a state institution. They were seldom visited by anyone. The care they received was impersonal. The anguish of their rejection and loneliness would be hard to describe.

Problems of old age and the care of the elderly are increasing constantly as medical advances prolong life. Most nursing homes have long waiting lists and the costs are prohibitive. A friend of ours who has been a nursing-home administrator, asked,

"Has it ever occurred to you what would happen if scientists do find a cure for cancer? We can't adequately care for the elderly now. What on earth would we do with them then?" She certainly wasn't against finding a cancer cure. It was a pragmatic query.

The care of the elderly is a problem that nearly everyone faces eventually. It's a pressing social need, but we don't usually give it much thought until we have to. Any form of limitation on our personal freedom grinds us, especially if we're "tied down" by elderly people. And, so, many people gladly put the aged in homes where they can be out of sight and out of mind.

"I think some of us neglect the elderly out of fear," someone remarked. "We're afraid to face the reality that someday we'll all be old, so we push it out of our minds and avoid associating with old people as much as possible."

"Doing your own thing" is a rallying call in our day which seems to have promoted selfishness, often at the expense of the elderly in our midst. The feeling is that the older generation is out of date. They just don't understand what's going on, so it's best to put them on a shelf. Dr. Daniel Boorstin, a historian for twenty-five years at the University of Chicago, was quoted in a newspaper interview on what he called "The reign of relevance: To teach only what is relevant, what is current, in the colleges, is to imprison man in the present. If we don't know what we have been capable of in the past, we can never be liberated in the future."[1]

Eastern cultures have a very different attitude toward age. When my father was in his 70's, having spent over fifty years in the Orient as a missionary, he received an invitation to join the staff of a Bible school in the Far East. They didn't want him just as a teacher. They felt that a man of his age and experience would add prestige to the school by his very presence! How different in our society when a person is forced to retire at sixty-five years of age because it's assumed that after that age he has little of value to contribute.

The Bible has many accounts of elderly people who accomplished memorable feats in their old age. Caleb was one of the few people in the older generation who were permitted to enter the promised land with Joshua. At the age of eighty-five he requested that he be allowed to claim the portion of land the Lord had promised him forty-five years earlier. After all, he had been a slave in Egypt, and had lived as a nomad in the desert with the rest of the nation for forty years. He was an old man and deserved to rest. But Caleb said, "I am still as strong to this day as I was in the day that Moses sent me; my strength now is as my strength was then, for war, and for going and coming. So now give me this hill country of which the LORD spoke on that day.[2] With Joshua's blessing and the Lord's help, Caleb won the conquest.

Someone has said that old age is the true revealer of character. As the face becomes wrinkled, the hair thin, the body bent, all that shows through is the character that has been in the making up to that point. The habit of Caleb's lifetime was that he "wholly followed the Lord." And when, as an aged man, he faced a hostile city, his God was still big enough to care for that problem.

Advancing age does not eliminate problems, nor does it make a person sweeter! Being old won't make me want to pray more, just because I have more time on my hands, if I haven't made a lifelong habit of prayer before. The same goes for Bible reading. If I am a demanding person now, I will still be a demanding person at seventy. If I am self-centered now, I will still be self-centered when I retire. Similarly, if I have formed habits of generosity, optimism and thoughtfulness now, they will be even more in evidence in later life. At seventy I will be all I have been becoming for seventy years.

Robert J. Little has defined age in this way: "I remain young as long as I can face each day as a fresh adventure with God."

According to this definition, one of the

"youngest" elderly people I know is a lady close to eighty who attends our church. Several years ago a stroke paralyzed her right side. She had always been right-handed but, with her right side virtually useless, she began using her left hand and discovered a latent skill in painting. She's our own "Grandma Moses." She has done numbers of lovely paintings and she is perpetually joyful. She didn't lie down and give up when life became hard. She looked for a different expression for her energies. Life is still an adventure for her.

"Preparation" for retirement almost always implies financial preparation. Put money in the bank. Buy stocks and bonds. Plan now for a source of income on which to live. Retirement benefits have become as important as the current salary in a new job. But I have rarely, if ever, heard any emphasis put on the preparation needed to build the character and spiritual stature necessary to withstand the unusual pressures inherent in old age. In the normal course of events, all of us will grow old. Now is not too soon to establish the habits of life that a frail or failing body cannot destroy.

I talked to an elderly couple who *had* made this kind of preparation. The husband had been retired from his business for a number of years. He and his wife bought a home in a warmer climate. Then, as advancing age curtailed their physical abilities, they decided to move into a church-run retirement complex. It's a place that can't even be considered by people who have no money in the bank. The retirement home offers the security of care for the rest of their lives. "We wanted it this way," they told me. "Now we won't be a burden to our children. Someone will always care for us even when we're no longer able to care for ourselves."

"Don't you miss the company of younger people?" I asked.

"Oh, certainly we do. That's one of the main disadvantages of living in a retirement home. But we make up for it by getting to church where we can be with young people."

"Are you happy?" I queried.

"Well, there's an adjustment to make," they admitted. "Some people never do adjust, and they complain all the time. But we have found that if we are friendly and happy, so are other people."

But what about the elderly who can't afford to buy their way into a pleasant, secure retirement home?

"Some of them live in places where rats wouldn't want to live!" exclaimed Marie, one of the women in a neighborhood Bible study who serves with her church one day a month with a "meals on wheels" program sponsored by a neighborhood house.

"I have been in homes you wouldn't believe," she went on. "With crumbling plaster, mud floors, bugs, filth. I was sick all day after my first experience in serving."

"Who do you serve with 'meals on wheels'?" I

asked.

"Well, first, we serve elderly people. Some are in their eighties and may be on waiting lists to get into nursing homes. We also serve hot meals to the blind, to crippled or bedridden people—to anyone who for some reason can't get out and shop for his own food.

"Who plans the meals?"

"The neighborhood house plans the menu and gives it to the church group which is coming that day to prepare it. We donate most of the food we bring. It's carried in portable ovens to keep it hot. For our day of serving, the children in our Sunday school make a decorative treat to put on each tray."

"Why do you keep going back if it made you sick to see people living in such miserable conditions?"

"I keep going back," Marie replied, "because I want to help. The people we serve get so lonely. They love to talk to their volunteers who come in. We can't stay long in each place if we're going to get the meals out while they're hot. But we can have short cheerful conversations which mean so much to them. In one home I ran into a former neighbor of ours. She had lost both her legs, and was so helpless and lonely. We both pulled out family pictures and reminisced of the 'old' days, and it brightened her day enormously, and mine, too. This is a small way in which I can serve God and express my love for him and for others,"

Marie concluded.

Helen is a registered nurse who heads a large community nursing service. Most of their patients are over sixty-five. "They need custodial care, companionship, conversation, as well as medicine and treatments," Helen commented.

"We, too, use volunteers to serve meals prepared by local hospitals for patients on special diets, such as diabetics. Many of the volunteers, though, are unwilling to do anything more than serve the meal and leave. I think this is where those of us in the profession can help lay people to understand the reasons for some of the behavior they see. People with certain diseases can't talk or smile. They may seem very unfriendly. Others fluctuate between laughing and crying. The uninitiated person is likely to take this sort of behavior personally."

Helen works under the same handicaps that seem to face most community service organizations today–lack of personnel and inadequate funds. "The medical welfare programs for the elderly sponsored by the government have created more problems than they have solved," she said. "We used to get financial support from such things as the community chest, but people don't give to that anymore. The general attitude is, 'Let the government pay for it.' But the government doesn't financially aid the kind of custodial care which is most needed."

"What do you think is the answer?" I asked.

"Well, quite frankly," Helen replied thoughtfully, "I think the basic human weakness is a spiritual one. Most people are selfish. They say, 'If it doesn't involve me directly, I'm not interested.' People need to have a spiritual awakening to be responsive to the needs of others. And I think the best place for this to happen is in the home. Children and young people should be excited about helping others. They can read to the elderly, or write letters for them. The reward is in the inner satisfaction of making life a little easier and happier for someone else." I knew what she was talking about. We had watched the weakening process of age take over my own father. And caring for him during the final months of his life in a large way involved our whole family.

It's so much easier to be objective about someone else's aged relative than your own. To watch someone who has been dynamic and strong and alert, an initiator of action, become increasingly dependent in every way, is not easy. Sometimes there are drastic personality and behavior changes which those closest to the individual often take personally. This is the time when family members need support and help in understanding and accepting the situation as a very normal process of physical deterioration. And, yet, most people are loath to even admit there is a problem, because somehow it seems such a disgrace!

A person is no less a person because he can no longer remember who he is or where he is. I believe with all my heart that we should treat the elderly with the same respect and dignity as we did when they were able to command it. Perhaps this is where the spiritual motivation is most needed, as Helen said.

God built the society, making the family its basic unit. The Bible commands us, "Honor your father and mother." For the young child this means obeying and submitting to parental authority. For the adult it means providing whatever love and care are necessary for the parents.

Jesus challenged the Pharisees and scribes on this very point when he said,

> "God's law is 'Honor your father and mother; anyone who reviles his parents must die.' But *you* say, 'Even if your parents are in need, you may give their support money to the church instead.' And so, by your man-made rule, you nullify the direct command of God to honor and care for your parents. You hypocrites! Well did Isaiah prophesy of you, 'These people say they honor Me, but their hearts are far away. Their worship is worthless, for they teach their man-made laws instead of those from God.' "[3]

Being lovingly responsible for your parents doesn't necessarily mean having them live with you. It does mean carefully and prayerfully doing what is best for all concerned. And if a nursing home is chosen, keep the welfare of the person constantly in mind. Being forgotten or neglected is something few of us can survive.

If a parent does live with one of his children, the other members of the family shouldn't feel that they no longer have any responsibility toward that parent. I have talked to many people who said something like this: "I was the one left holding the bag. I took care of mother. When she became senile and could never be left alone, I would have loved to get away for a day or two. But my brothers and sisters resented it if I even asked for a few hours."

A local church should be just as sensitive to the needs of its elderly people as with its youth programs. "I would like to see Christians go into the nursing home business," said a woman who had herself held a responsible position in a nursing home. "I have worked in a nursing home where the primary aim was to make money. A mercenary perspective has no compassion, no heart. Why, I have seen a patient denied the use of an extra towel because 'the room she is paying for allows only one towel a day'! We need nursing homes that are run out of love—where each person is made to feel needed and wanted, places reasonable enough for lower incomes."

The use of foster homes for elderly people who have no families is a growing venture. Young families would be enriched if they would invite elderly people over for dinner. We had a widow in our home one Sunday who had lived in our community for sixty years. She held our children spellbound for almost two hours as she described what the town was like when she was a child and how it had changed and grown over the years.

"Grandpa's a cool guy," was our teen-ager's matter-of-fact comment after listening to my father reminisce of missionary experience in China one afternoon.

We considered it a privilege to have my dad at home until the day he died. We watched him slow down physically. But his spirit and sense of humor didn't ever dim. Even after he had a severe fall and was unconscious for a while, when he regained consciousness he made a comical comment which immediately relieved the tension. When he became bedridden the children would run up to his room to see him, to hold his hand, to talk to him. Our youngest would climb right over the siderails to give him a big hug and kiss.

There were days during his last month when my mother and I thought we wouldn't make it through another day. One afternoon a friend came to "grandpa-sit" just so my mother and I could get relief. Her own mother had died recently. She was sensitive to our need. Dad preached to her in Chinese for four hours, and she loved it! One priceless nurse stayed with him the last five nights he lived. She gave him loving professional care as a service to the Lord.

Dad died at home just as the school bell rang to send the children home for lunch. All four of our children wanted to see Grandpa; he had been so much a part of their lives. Our ten-year-old son stood quietly by his bed for a few moments. Then he turned and took his grandma's hand and, without any tears, said, "Grandpa's so much better now. He won't be falling anymore like he used to." They had learned to accept his failing strength. They accepted his death, as it was indeed, a blessing from God. These are lessons that have the greatest impact when they are learned firsthand.

Dad enriched our lives to the very end. We lost nothing. We're grateful for every memory we have of him. He could have echoed the words of the psalmist, "O God, You have helped me from my earliest childhood. . . . And now that I am old and gray, don't forsake me. Give me time to tell this new generation (and their children too) about all Your mighty miracles."[4]

10

". . . and my neighbor as myself"

"This is the first sensible thing I've seen the church do in twenty years," was the comment of a man when first introduced to an organization named the Fish.

The Fish is a lay organization which has sprung up in communities all over the world. It is made up of volunteers whose slogan is "Love thy neighbor." The idea had its roots in England and then spread to the United States and elsewhere.

Ann, my suburban friend who manages to teach released-time classes, take foster children and care for her own family, is also the prime mover of the Fish organization in her community.

I asked her, "How did you get started?"

"We began," she said, "with eight people who were willing to volunteer their time and services. A volunteer usually offers to be on call for one twenty-four-hour period per month. The next item was to set up a phone-answering service which would take calls around the clock. After that we passed out handbills in the community which said, 'When you need help, call this number.' "

"What kind of help do you give?" I asked.

"We take elderly people or shut-ins to the store or doctor's office, read to the blind, provide emergency baby-sitting, or a hot meal for a family if the mother is ill, or referral service when professional help is needed—just about anything you could think of. For instance, last night the police called me and said they had an ill alcoholic, and would I help him? The local hospital had no room except for emergencies. Next I phoned a rescue mission about twenty miles away. They said, 'We'll take him if he can walk in and take a shower.' I phoned the police station again and this time talked to the sick man himself. He asked, 'Are you going to save me?' I replied, 'I'm sure going to try!' And he began to cry. My husband and another man picked him up at the police station and drove him to the mission." Ann went on. "One Fish volunteer who was on call phoned me the other day. She said, 'I have a call from a little old lady who has just been released from the hospital. She needs her hair washed and set. Who do I call to do it?' 'You,' I replied."

"There was a hesitant 'OK' before the volunteer hung up. Later a very jubilant young woman phoned back to tell me what a rewarding experience it had been to shampoo an old lady's hair!"

Fish volunteers in another community kept a home with five small children functioning–preparing meals, doing laundry, cleaning–while the young mother was hospitalized for several months with terminal cancer. They kept up their help until after the difficult transition was made following her death and the father had the home going on his own.

The Rev. Robert Howell, an Episcopal minister who spearheaded the Fish movement in the United States, said,

> The purpose of this whole program is to demonstrate God's love for His people through us, His church. . . . We say with St. Paul that the church is the body of Christ. If it is truly His hands and His feet, then, true to its Head, it will find itself much involved in the lives of people who are sick or unhappy and troubled. That has always been characteristic of Christ. . . . [The Fish volunteer] needs to be so fortified with the solid meaty substance of faith that he can feed others who are hungry.[1]

It isn't enough to be a "do-gooder." Emphasizing Christ's second commandment, "You shall love your neighbor as yourself," and excluding the first commandment, "You shall love the Lord your God with all your heart, and with all your soul, and with all your mind, and with all your strength,"[2] is like putting the cart before the horse. The first establishes the relationship which is absolutely essential to the fulfilling of the second. If we love God with all our being, we are better able to love people as we should.

In the past several months I have talked with scores of people in all kinds of places. I have been to the local office of the government-sponsored poverty program, and learned there were five hundred people in our community alone who lacked an adequate diet. Part of the program of this office was to find jobs for people and also to train people to fill jobs that were available.

I spent an afternoon helping to distribute food supplements to needy families. The local poverty office was trying to meet their food needs to keep them going. Other families were suffering because of prolonged strikes, or workers had been laid off their jobs. A local church decided to help the hungry by making an arrangement with a local supermarket that for every purchase a church member made, the food store would match it. Members of the congregation filled six Volkswagon buses with their purchases for the poor in their community. The supermarket matched their gifts.

I visited a school for handicapped children. Most of them would not go very far in formal education, but they could be trained for certain job skills. The school was spotless and shiny in every corner. This was the responsibility of one of the school graduates and he rightly took great pride in his work. "We could use volunteer help—people who are willing to sit in the classroom as teachers' helpers," said the principal. "Some disturbed children need a comforting lap to sit on. In past years it seemed that people were far more willing to give of themselves and their time, to help others. Now they're more interested in knowing, 'What's in it for me?' "

I talked to a police officer who is anxious to improve police-community relations. He said, "It's much better to establish communication in the community *before* law enforcement is needed than *after.* But this means more policemen are needed to mingle in the community, and people aren't willing to pay the price in taxes for that. It's also interesting to note that very often the people who are afraid of crime in the streets and riots, and who cry the loudest for greater police protection, are the same people who cuss out the officer when given a ticket. The law is OK as long as it's leveled at the other guy but not at me! Society is plagued by selfishness—me and my rights—but couldn't care less about the other person."

"How would you like to see the community improve its relations with law-enforcement officials?" I asked.

"The best thing any community can do to help the police," he replied, "is to have self-respect. If a person thinks enough of himself to bear his own share of responsibilities in a free society, both his rights and the other person's will be protected.

Also, the community should think enough of itself to see that policemen are chosen and promoted on the basis of their capability and not on the basis of political patronage or seniority. Policemen are human. They make mistakes. They have to be mature enough to treat people on the basis of their actions, not on how they might feel toward the person at the moment."

I have listened to many thinking young people who are deeply disturbed by the dualism which allows Christians to piously sing on Sunday, "Take my life and let it be, consecrated Lord to Thee, Take my silver and my gold, not a mite would I withhold," and then on Monday close their hands to the needy. This is one of the many factors that has given rise to the spirit of nihilism and despair so prevalent among thinking young people. One such college junior said, "I reject the Establishment and its biased attitudes by ignoring its people." It is good to know of men such as Dr. Francis Schaeffer, who are carrying intellectual "cups of cold water" to thoughtful questioning youth.

I have seen Christian marriages in deep trouble because marriage partners are more interested in what they are getting out of the relationship than what they are putting in. So often they are immature people playing a role, not willing to face themselves or life as it really is.

I have met women who feel that being "just a housewife" is too demeaning. They feel they were created for a higher purpose than that. This was the sentiment expressed by one lady I talked to who had become involved in the Women's Liberation Movement.

I have sat in on a psychiatric seminar and watched a team of about fifteen psychologists and assorted therapists strip away layer by layer the past history of a patient. I have seen the tension build until the patient paced the floor and the parents were deeply upset, and it was as though everyone in the room viewed the gradual unveiling of a live bomb and said, "There it is, folks. A real live bomb. Isn't it a shame none of us knows how to defuse it!" Here was a group who were masters at exposing a person's past, capable of putting their diagnostic fingers on the causes of present behavior. But they were powerless to change the past, to help people forgive, to change their way of life to cope with the present and the future. And so over and over again the process would be repeated—the careful exposure of the live bomb; the failure to defuse it. And unless someone could do something, that bomb just might explode.

I have watched people disintegrate emotionally and psychologically because they could not face themselves and accept the responsibility for their actions. In their lives it was always easier to blame someone else and to remain permanently crippled.

I have been in the homes of the bereaved—those who have mourned the death of a child, a husband, a father. The Bible says,

"It is better to go to the house of mourning than to go to the house of feasting; for this is the end of all men, and the living will lay it to heart."[3] When we face death realistically we are more likely to face life realistically.

I have walked through our community and looked at the dying elms, broken windows, boarded-up stores and theaters. I have smelled the air heavy with pollution. I have listened to voices of despair, cries of belligerence, demanding people calling for justice without compassion, hysterical voices responding to emotion rather than reason. They are outward signs of an inner decay—an awesome, horrible disease that no one can seem to stop.

My purely human reaction is to run—to move way out into a place of quiet, gorgeous scenery, clear air, no people, no problems, just serenity. But just when my mind pushes into high gear with such thoughts, the Lord reminds me of Titus, a young man doing a vital job in a rotten place called Crete. The Cretans said of themselves that they were "always liars, evil beasts, lazy gluttons." Their island wasn't the choicest place to live on earth, and I'm sure Titus would gladly have gone elsewhere to serve God. But Paul reminded him that this was exactly why he had asked Titus to remain in Crete, to "amend what was defective. For the grace of God has appeared for the salvation of *all* men [even Cretans]."[4]

One of the most alarming voices to which I

have listened in recent months has been that of the evangelical Christian cutting to ribbons his fellow Christian. The conservative evangelical makes caustic remarks about the Christian who has departed from the fundamentalist fold, and the more "open-minded" Christian, in turn, throws equally strong language at his conservative brother. The truly frightening thing is the level of hostility justified by Christians as preserving the purity of "the truth."

The Bible speaks in rather strong language about this: "Anyone who says he is walking in the light of Christ but hates his brother Christian is still in darkness."[5] Christ said that the mark of his true followers was their love for one another.

The Old Testament prophet Hosea said the problem with God's people was that they had tuned God out. They weren't listening to him. "My people are destroyed because they don't know Me," said the Lord.[6] The land of that day was filled with sadness, violence, adultery, air and water pollution. Hosea, too, would probably have loved to have gotten away from it all, but God called on him to stay not only in a disintegrating society but in a disastrous marriage as well. God reached his people through Hosea with a message of love. Hosea loved a woman who deserted him. His love moved him to scour the slums for her. His love involved his whole life. It was this man, who had demonstrated such love in his own home, who could compassionately say to his people, "Come back to God. Live by the principles of love and justice, and always be expecting much from Him, your God."[7]

God's own people need to repent. The Lord told the nation of Israel that their welfare as a people depended upon their relationship to God:

"If my people who are called by my name humble themselves, and pray and seek my face, and turn from their wicked ways, then I will hear from heaven, and will forgive their sin and heal their land."[8]

All our praying won't mean much unless there is genuine repentance as well, a recognition that change is needed. Then I ask, How far am I willing to be motivated by the love of God? This is where the first commandment of establishing a right relationship with God is all-important. And because I love the Lord, I will love my neighbor. If I don't love my neighbor, it shows I don't love the Lord either. Christ's love moves me to give myself unselfishly to him and to give of myself to others. I give not because I can afford it, but because I love so much that the cost doesn't matter.

Am I willing to pay the price of extending myself to the people around me? To adequately meet people's needs takes money (lots of it), manpower, faith, prayer, commitment, love.

And it works. If you walked through our town and saw only the decay, you wouldn't be seeing the whole picture.

Listen to the president of a teacher's college in

the town next to ours which suffered enormous loss to its buildings in a recent fire: "As the Phillips' translation of 2 Corinthians 4:9 puts it, we are 'knocked down, but not knocked out.' Our confidence is in a living Lord, who has a living heart to love us, a living eye to see our needs, and a living, almighty hand to help us."[9]

Next, I would like you to come with me through the door of a nearby convent. It is part of a large parish. The nuns who live there are primarily teachers in the school run by the parish. Most of them wear street clothes instead of habits. The building is modern, neat, comfortable.

Inside, a group of about ten nuns assembled in a few minutes and we went to the recreation room, gathered chairs in a circle, and had a Bible study.

A few days earlier these nuns were doing house-to-house visitation in their parish community. In the course of making their calls two of them came to the home of some ladies who regularly attend a neighborhood Bible study.[10] The conversation quickly turned to the subject of Bible studies, and the two sisters asked one question after another with avid interest. The discussion ended with the nuns inviting the ladies to visit the convent, and saying, "I think the Lord brought us here today."

It was that contact that had led Rosemarie, one of the ladies in that home, and me to the convent. Before we started the Bible study, one of the nuns told of the spontaneous prayer meetings and Bible studies they had started among themselves.

"One night, at midnight," Sister Mary Ann related, "I just felt like praying with someone. So a few of us got together and prayed and read the Bible. It was wonderful!"

One nun said that their relationships with each other had improved since they were praying together. Evidently nuns are quite human, and living together within the walls of a convent doesn't guarantee perfect harmony! Christ was improving their interpersonal relationships.

We began our study with sentence prayers all around the circle. They were warm, spontaneous, unclichéd prayers. We opened our New Testaments to Mark 1 and the discussion was lively and refreshing. After we were through, one nun commented, "I have read that passage many times, but today I received insights into it that I have never had before."

Another said, "It's that commitment to Christ which is the real hang-up, isn't it?" It wasn't a negative comment, just an honest observation that all of us find it hard to give up ourselves and commit our lives by faith to Jesus Christ.

"It's even more amazing," interjected another nun, "when you realize that the disciples whom Jesus called didn't know him that well. Yet they left everything to follow him."

The openness and honesty and warmth of this group of sisters toward the Scriptures and to each other and to us as "outsiders" was astonishing. It was as though the Lord allowed that door to be opened to let us glimpse the beautiful thing he was doing. Rosemarie and I left the convent so exhilarated by what we had seen and heard that there just weren't words big enough to give the Lord the praise we felt in our hearts. God is at work in our community, changing people's lives, and using changed people who really love him to show his love to others.

However, I have discovered that being involved in a neighborhood Bible-study group is not necessarily a substitute for social action. We need to be both "contemplative" and actively involved in the lives and needs of others. In fact, a Bible-study group gives an excellent frame of reference for social action to take place. We become sensitive to one another's needs. And the Word of God and Christ's love move us to purposeful action.

Do you see that black teen-age girl riding her bike? She is on her way two miles across town carrying homemade rolls hot out of the oven to the home of those white people over there. Someone in their family just died. The girl's mother is in a neighborhood Bible-study group.

See those ladies carrying a vacuum cleaner to that house? Someone is sick in there, and they are going to clean. They weren't asked to go. They just went. They're in a Bible-study group too.

That Christian lady speaks Spanish and sponsors programs for Latin people in our area.

Then look. There's a member of a Bible study

taking a friend to the doctor. She sprained her ankle and had no transportation.

That big box is filled with food for a family whose father is in the veteran's hospital. The food was donated by women in a Bible-study group.

Would you believe it? Husbands get in the act too! That man is carrying a big pipe to help a fellow church member fix his plumbing, and there's a man helping his neighbor paint his house.

Another husband is on his way in the middle of the night to take care of four small children while the parents go to the hospital for number five.

That lady is a Christian teacher. She is tutoring a child having educational problems.

There goes a young woman to donate three afternoons a week to teach typing at the job-training center. She's in a Bible study too.

There's another Christian woman going to the League of Women Voters' meeting.

Small groups of people are meeting all over our community, brought together by the Word of God, motivated by the love of Christ and genuine love and concern for each other, moving out and touching other people's lives with Christ's love.

It was Sister Mary Ann who said, "I cannot be pessimistic about what I see in the world. The Lord is doing such exciting things!"

God doesn't expect everyone to do everything. But he does expect each of us to do something. An insignificant rod in Moses' hand became an instrument of God's power to move the nation of Israel out of slavery in Egypt. What has God put in *your* hand? Are you using it?

In the Old Testament the Lord said to the religious establishment of that day, "I'm not interested in the religious ritual you go through, because you still quarrel and fight and oppress people and live as you please." Rather,

> Is not this the fast that choose: to loose the bonds of wickedness, to undo the thongs of the yoke, to let the oppressed go free, and to break every yoke? Is it not to share your bread with the hungry, and bring the homeless poor into your house; when you see the naked, to cover him, and not to hide yourself from your own flesh? *Then* shall your light break forth like the dawn, and your healing shall spring up speedily.[11]

The lesson of the New Testament is the same: "Let us stop just *saying* we love people; let us *really* love them, and *show it* by our *actions.*"[12]

I had a classmate in nurse's training who went to Africa with her husband as a missionary. She gave herself freely in her roles as a wife, a mother, a nurse, a friend to the nationals. A few hours after the birth of her fourth child, she died. The Africans flocked in to mourn her death. The most eloquent eulogy came from the lips of an African woman who said, quite simply, "She loved."

notes

Chapter 1

[1] James 1:22-25, RSV.
[2] Eccles. 9:10, RSV.

Chapter 2

[1] Matt. 12:34-37, RSV.
[2] Luke 4:22, RSV.
[3] James 1:20, RSV.
[4] Matt. 26:11, RSV.
[5] Mark 12:31, RSV.
[6] James 2:14-17, Living Letters.

Chapter 3

[1] Acts 1:8, RSV.
[2] Acts 1:11, Living N.T.
[3] Acts 1:14, RSV.
[4] Acts 2:4, Living N.T.
[5] Acts 2:40, RSV.
[6] Acts 2:42, RSV.
[7] Col. 3:8-17, Living N.T.
[8] Heb. 10:34.
[9] Rom. 12:13, RSV.
[10] 1 Pet. 4:9, RSV.

Chapter 4

[1]Hubert H. Humphrey, *The Challenge of Our Cities* (Washington, D.C.: U.S. Govt. Printing Office, 1967). Bulletin No. O-275-396.

[2]Ibid.

[3]Howard Hageman, "Will Evangelicals Penetrate the Inner City?" *Eternity* (Jan., 1970), pp. 23-24.

[4]Acts 3:6, Living N.T.

[5]Acts 3:7.

[6]Jer. 1:1, 11-12, RSV.

Chapter 5

[1]1 Cor. 4:20, Living N.T.

[2]2 Tim. 4:11.

[3]Matt. 25:36, 40, RSV.

[4]2 Tim. 1:16, Living N.T.

Chapter 6

[1]Michael Haynes, "Three Minutes to Midnight: The Evangelical and Racism," *Evangelical Mission Quarterly* (Fall, 1968), pp. 2-3.

[2]James Baldwin, *The Fire Next Time* (New York: Dial, 1963), p. 21.

[3]Eph. 2:14-15, Living N.T.

[4]Rom. 12:17, 21, Living N.T.

Chapter 7

[1]Prov. 16:33, RSV.

[2]Dan. 5:21, Living Prophecies.

[3]Rom. 13:1, Living N.T.

[4]Eph. 5:13, RSV.

[5]Malcolm X and Alex Haley, *The Autobiography of Malcolm X* (New York: Grove, 1966), p. 205.

[6]Klaas Runia, "Evangelical Responsibility in a Secularized Society," *Christianity Today* (June 19, 1970), pp. 11-14.

[7]Gen. 50:20, RSV.

[8]John B. Anderson, "Principles for Participation in Politics" in "Christians in Politics," *Theology Today* (Jan., 1970), pp. 379-80.

[9]Ibid.

[10]Mark O. Hatfield, "The Path to Peace" in "Christians in Politics," *Theology Today* (Jan., 1970), p. 397.

Chapter 8

[1]Prov. 22:6.

[2]1 Sam. 3:1, RSV.

[3]Prov. 16:7, RSV.

[4]Rom. 12:1, Phillips.

[5]Prov. 1:33; 2:6-9, RSV.

Chapter 9

[1]*The Chicago Daily News* (May, 1970).

[2]Josh. 14:11-12, RSV.

[3]Matt. 15:4-9, Living N.T.

[4]Psalm 71:17-18, Living Psalms.

Chapter 10

[1]Robert L. Howell, *Fish–For My People* (New York: Morehouse, 1968), pp. 45, 60, 86.

[2]Mark 12:30-31, RSV.

[3]Eccles. 7:2, RSV.

[4]Titus 1:5; 2:11, RSV.

[5]1 John 2:9, Living N.T.

[6]Hos. 4:6, Living Prophecies.

[7]Hos. 12:6, Living Prophecies.

[8]2 Chron. 7:14, RSV.

[9]Dr. Martin Koehneke, President, Concordia Teachers College, Letter to friends and alumni of the college (May 18, 1970).

[10]For the story of these neighborhood Bible-study groups and how they started, read the author's book, *Caught with My Mouth Open* (Wheaton, Ill.: Shaw, 1969).

[11]Isa. 58:6-8, RSV.

[12]1 John 3:18, Living N.T.